CONTRACT

CONTRACT
FOURTH EDITION

Alison Smith

This edition published 2024 by
The University of Law
2 Bunhill Row
London EC1Y 8HQ

© The University of Law 2024

All rights reserved. No part of this publication may be reproduced, stored in a retrieval system, or transmitted, in any form or by any means, without the prior written permission of the copyright holder, application for which should be addressed to the publisher.

Contains public sector information licensed under the Open Government Licence v3.0

British Library Cataloguing in Publication Data

A catalogue record for this book is available from the British Library.

ISBN 978 1 80502 120 9

Preface

This book is part of a series of Study Manuals that have been specially designed to support the reader to achieve the SQE1 Assessment Specification in relation to Functioning Legal Knowledge. Each Study Manual aims to provide the reader with a solid knowledge and understanding of fundamental legal principles and rules, including how those principles and rules might be applied in practice.

This Study Manual covers the Solicitors Regulation Authority's syllabus for the SQE1 assessment for Contract in a concise and tightly focused manner. The Manual provides a clear statement of relevant legal rules and a well-defined road map through examinable law and practice. The Manual aims to bring the law and practice to life through the use of example scenarios based on realistic client-based problems and allows the reader to test their knowledge and understanding through single best answer questions that have been modelled on the SRA's sample assessment questions.

For those readers who are students at the University of Law, the Study Manual is used alongside other learning resources and the University's assessment bank to best prepare students not only for the SQE1 assessments, but also for a future life in professional legal practice.

We hope that you find the Study Manual supportive of your preparation for SQE1 and we wish you every success.

The legal principles and rules contained within this Manual are stated as at 1 May 2024.

Author acknowledgments
Alison would like to thank Jan McEwan and Russell Binch for reviewing and commenting on the content of chapters and sample questions: their input was invaluable.

Contents

Preface		v
Table of Cases		xiii
Table of Statutes		xv
PART 1	**FORMATION**	**1**
Chapter 1	**Agreement**	**3**
	SQE1 syllabus	3
	Learning outcomes	3
	1.1 Introduction	4
	1.2 Offers and invitations to treat	4
	1.2.1 Goods on display	5
	1.2.2 Advertisements	5
	1.2.3 Auctions and tenders	6
	1.3 Acceptance	7
	1.3.1 Definition	7
	1.3.2 Communication of acceptance	7
	1.3.3 Acceptance by post	8
	1.4 Termination of offers	9
	1.4.1 Rejection	10
	1.4.2 Revocation	10
	1.4.3 Lapse of time	11
	1.5 Certainty and completeness	11
	Summary	12
	Sample questions	13
Chapter 2	**Intention to Create Legal Relations**	**17**
	SQE1 syllabus	17
	Learning outcomes	17
	2.1 Introduction	18
	2.2 Commercial agreements	18
	2.3 Domestic agreements	19
	Summary	20
	Sample question	20

Chapter 3 — Consideration — 21

SQE1 syllabus		21
Learning outcomes		21
3.1	Identifying consideration	22
	3.1.1 Consideration need not be adequate	22
	3.1.2 Consideration must be sufficient	22
	3.1.3 Past consideration	23
	3.1.4 Consideration – summary	24
3.2	Contractual variations	24
3.3	Alteration promises to pay more	24
	3.3.1 Alteration promises to pay more – summary	26
3.4	Alteration promises to accept less	26
	3.4.1 Rule in *Pinnel's Case*	26
	3.4.2 Promissory estoppel	27
	3.4.3 Alteration promises to accept less – summary	28
Summary		28
Sample questions		29

Chapter 4 — Parties — 33

SQE1 syllabus		33
Learning outcomes		33
4.1	Introduction	34
4.2	Privity of contract	34
4.3	Contracts (Rights of Third Parties) Act 1999	34
4.4	Agency	35
	4.4.1 Actual authority	35
	4.4.2 Apparent authority	36
Summary		37
Sample questions		38

Chapter 5 — Capacity — 41

SQE1 syllabus		41
Learning outcomes		41
5.1	Introduction	42
5.2	Minors	42
5.3	Mental incapacity	43
5.4	Corporations	43
	5.4.1 Registered companies	43
	5.4.2 Statutory corporations	44
	5.4.3 Limited liability partnerships	44

	Summary	44
	Sample question	44
PART 2	**CONTENTS**	**47**
Chapter 6	**Contents**	**49**
	SQE1 syllabus	49
	Learning outcomes	49
	6.1 Express terms	50
	6.1.1 Incorporation of terms	50
	6.1.2 Classification of terms	51
	6.2 Implied terms	54
	6.2.1 Terms implied at common law	54
	6.2.2 Terms implied by statute	55
	Summary	59
	Sample questions	60
Chapter 7	**Exemption Clauses**	**63**
	SQE1 syllabus	63
	Learning outcomes	63
	7.1 Introduction	64
	7.2 Common law rules	64
	7.2.1 Incorporation	64
	7.2.2 Construction	64
	7.3 Statutory controls	65
	7.3.1 Unfair Contract Terms Act 1977	65
	7.3.2 Consumer Rights Act 2015	68
	7.4 Exemption clauses and third parties	69
	Summary	70
	Sample questions	71
PART 3	**REMEDIES**	**75**
Chapter 8	**Damages**	**77**
	SQE1 syllabus	77
	Learning outcomes	77
	8.1 Introduction	78
	8.2 Expectation and reliance loss	78
	8.3 Types of loss recoverable	80
	8.4 Remoteness of damage	80
	8.5 Mitigation of loss	82

	8.6	Quantification of damages	82
	8.7	Specified damages and penalty clauses	83
		8.7.1 The distinction between a specified (or liquidated) damages clause and a penalty clause	83
		8.7.2 How does the court decide whether the clause is a specified damages clause or a penalty clause?	84
	Summary		84
	Sample questions		85
Chapter 9	**Equitable and Other Remedies**		**87**
	SQE1 syllabus		87
	Learning outcomes		87
	9.1	Remedies that make the defendant perform the contract	88
		9.1.1 Action for an agreed sum	88
		9.1.2 Specific performance	88
		9.1.3 Injunction	88
	9.2	Restitution	89
		9.2.1 Recovery of money paid where there has been a total failure of consideration	89
		9.2.2 Compensation for work done or goods supplied	90
		9.2.3 Restitutionary damages	91
	9.3	Guarantees	92
	9.4	Indemnities	93
	Summary		94
	Sample questions		94
PART 4	**TERMINATION**		**97**
Chapter 10	**Termination**		**99**
	SQE1 syllabus		99
	Learning outcomes		99
	10.1	Termination	100
	10.2	Frustration	101
		10.2.1 What constitutes frustration	101
		10.2.2 Consequences of frustration	104
		10.2.3 Frustration – summary	106
	10.3	Discharge by performance	106
		10.3.1 Exceptions	106
	Summary		109
	Sample questions		110

PART 5		**VITIATING FACTORS**	113
Chapter 11		**Misrepresentation**	115
	SQE1 syllabus		115
	Learning outcomes		115
	11.1	Introduction	116
	11.2	Categories of pre-contract statements	116
	11.3	Definition of misrepresentation	118
		11.3.1 An untrue statement	118
		11.3.2 A statement of fact, not opinion or future intention	118
		11.3.3 Statement must be made by one contracting party to the other	119
		11.3.4 The statement must induce the other party into entering into the contract	119
	11.4	Types of misrepresentation and damages	119
		11.4.1 Fraudulent misrepresentation	119
		11.4.2 Negligent misrepresentation	120
		11.4.3 Innocent misrepresentation	120
	11.5	Rescission	121
	Summary		123
	Sample questions		124
Chapter 12		**Duress and Undue Influence**	127
	SQE1 syllabus		127
	Learning outcomes		127
	12.1	Introduction	128
	12.2	Duress	128
		12.2.1 Effect of duress	129
		12.2.2 Link between economic duress and consideration	130
	12.3	Undue influence	131
		12.3.1 Actual and presumed undue influence	131
		12.3.2 Undue influence and the position of third parties	133
	Summary		136
	Sample questions		137
Chapter 13		**Mistake and Illegality**	141
	SQE1 syllabus		141
	Learning outcomes		141
	13.1	Mistake	142
		13.1.1 Common mistake	142
		13.1.2 Cross-purpose mistake	143
		13.1.3 Unilateral mistake	143
		13.1.4 Mistake or misrepresentation?	145

13.2	Illegal contracts	146
	13.2.1 Contracts illegal under statute	147
	13.2.2 Contracts illegal at common law	147
	13.2.3 Covenants in restraint of trade	147
Summary		148
Sample questions		148
Glossary		151
Index		155

Table of Cases

A	Adler v Dickson [1955] 1 QB 158	69
	Anglia Television v Reed [1972] 1 QB 60 (CA)	80
	Ashmore, Benson, Pease & Co Ltd v AV Dawson Ltd [1973] 1 WLR 828	146
	Atlas Express v Kafco [1989] 1 All ER 641	130
	Attorney-General v Blake [2001] 1 AC 268	91
B	Barry v Davies [2000] 1 WLR 1962	6–7, 14
	Bell v Lever Bros [1932] AC 161	143
	Blackpool & Fylde Aero Club Ltd v Blackpool Borough Council [1990] 1 WLR 1195 (CA)	7
	Brimnes, The [1975] QB 929	10
	British Steel Corp v Cleveland Bridge and Engineering Co Ltd [1984] 1 All ER 504	91
	Butler Machine Tool Co Ltd v Ex-Cell-O Corporation (England) Ltd [1979] 1 WLR 401	8
C	Car & Universal Finance v Caldwell [1964] 1 All ER 290	122
	Carlill v Carbolic Smoke Ball Company [1893] 1 QB 256 (CA)	5–6, 11
	Carillion Construction Ltd v Felix (UK) Ltd [2001] BLR 1	128
	Casey's Patents, Re [1892] 1 Ch 669	23, 31
	Cavendish Square Holding BV v Makdessi; ParkingEye Ltd v Beavis [2015] 3 WLR 1373	84
	Central London Property Trust v High Trees House [1947] KB 130	27
	Credit Lyonnais Bank Nederland v Burch [1997] 1 All ER 144	135
	Crystal Palace FC (2000) Ltd v Iain Dowie [2007] EWHC 1392(QB)	122
	Cundy v Lindsay (1878) 3 App Cas 459	144
D	Daniel v Drew [2005] EWCA Civ 507	131, 139
E	East v Maurer [1991] 2 All ER 733	119–120, 124
	Esso Petroleum v Commissioners of Customs and Excise [1976] 1 WLR 1	18–19
F	Foakes v Beer (1884) 9 App Cas 605	26
H	Holwell Securities Ltd v Hughes [1974] 1 WLR 155 (CA)	8
	Hong Kong Fir Shipping Co Ltd v Kawasaki Kisen Kaisha Ltd [1962] 2 QB (CA)	53
	Howard Marine & Dredging v Ogden [1978] 2 All ER 1134 (CA)	120
J	Jarvis v Swans Tours [1973] 1 QB 233 (CA)	80
L	Leaf v International Galleries [1950] 2 KB 86	121–122
	Lewis v Averay [1972] 1 QB 198	145

Table of Cases

M
Metropolitan Water Board v Dick Kerr [1918] AC 119 — 103
Mountford v Scott [1975] 1 All ER 198 — 10

N
North Ocean Shipping v Hyundai Construction (The Atlantic Baron) [1979] QB 705 — 129

O
O'Sullivan v Management Agency Ltd [1985] QB 428 — 132

P
Page One Records v Britton [1968] WLR 157 — 89
Parsons (Livestock) Ltd v Uttley Ingham [1978] 1 QB 791 — 81
Pinnel's Case — 26, 30
Proform Sports Management Ltd v Proactive Sports Management [2006] EWHC 2903 (Ch) — 43

R
Raffles v Wickelhaus (1864) 2 Hurl & C 906 — 143
Royal Bank of Scotland v Etridge (No 2) [2001] 4 All ER 449 — 134
Ruxley Electronics v Forsyth [1996] AC 344 — 83

S
Scammell v Ouston [1941] AC 251 (HL) — 11
Spice Girls v Aprilia World Service BV [2000] EMLR 748 — 118
St John Shipping Corp. v Joseph Rank Ltd [1957] 1 QB 267 — 146
Sumpter v Hedges [1898] 1 QB 673 — 108, 110
Super Servant Two, The [1990] 1 Lloyd's Rep 1 — 104

T
Tweddle v Atkinson (1861) 1 B & S 393 — 34

W
Watteau v Fenwick [1893] 1 QB 346 — 39
Williams v Roffey Bros & Nicholls [1991] 1 QB 1 — 25, 29, 130
Wrotham Park Estate v Parkside Homes [1974] 1 WLR 798 — 92

Table of Statutes

C	Companies Act 2006	43
	s 31	43
	s 39	43
	s 40(1)	43
	Competition Act 1998	147
	Consumer Rights Act 2015	57, 65, 70
	s 9	68, 73, 57, 58, 59, 62
	s 10	68, 73, 57, 58, 59, 62
	s 11	57, 58, 59, 68
	s 17	57, 145
	s 19	58
	s 20	58, 62
	s 22	58, 62
	s 23	58, 62
	s 24	58
	s 31	68, 73
	s 49	57, 58, 59, 69
	s 50	69
	s 51	57, 69
	s 52	57, 59, 69
	s 54	59
	s 57	69
	Contracts (Rights of Third Parties) Act 1999	33, 69, 70
	s 1(1)(a)	34
	s 1(1)(b)	34
	s 1(2)	34
L	Law Reform (Frustrated Contracts) Act 1943	106, 109
	s 1(2)	104-105, 112
	s 1(3)	105, 112,
	Limited Liability Partnerships Act 2000	44
M	Misrepresentation Act 1967	
	s 2(1)	120-121, 123-124
S	Sale of Goods Act 1979	42, 60, 73
	s 12	56, 144
	s 12(1)	55
	s 13	56, 66
	s 13(1)	55
	s 14	55, 56, 66
	s 14(2)	55
	s 14(2A)	55
	s 14(3)	55
	s 57	14
	s 57(2)	6

Table of Statutes

	Supply of Goods and Services Act 1982	55, 56
	s 2(1)	56
	s 3	56, 66
	s 4	66, 71
	s 4(2)	56
	s 4(5)	56
	s 13	56, 61, 66, 70, 71, 107, 108, 57
	s 14	56, 57
	s 15	57
U	Unfair Contract Terms Act 1977	63, 67, 110
	s 2	66
	s 2(1)	65, 66, 70
	s 2(2)	66, 70, 71
	s 3	65, 72, 104
	s 6	66
	s 6(1)(a)	65
	s 7	66, 71
	s 7(3A)	65
	Sch 2	67, 68

PART 1
FORMATION

1 Agreement

1.1	Introduction	4
1.2	Offers and invitations to treat	4
1.3	Acceptance	7
1.4	Termination of offers	9
1.5	Certainty and completeness	11

SQE1 syllabus

This chapter will enable you to achieve the SQE1 assessment specification in relation to functioning legal knowledge of the core principles of agreement (comprising an offer that has been accepted). Agreement is one of the three essential elements of a binding contract. The other two elements needed for a contract are intention to create legal relations (**Chapter 2**) and consideration (**Chapter 3**).

Note that, for SQE1, candidates are not usually required to recall specific case names or cite statutory or regulatory authorities. Cases are provided for illustrative purposes only.

Learning outcomes

By the end of this chapter you will be able to apply relevant core legal principles and rules appropriately and effectively, at the level of a competent newly qualified solicitor in practice, to realistic client-based and ethical problems and situations in the following areas:

- recognising when an offer has been made;
- establishing when an offer has been accepted to reach an agreement;
- recognising when an offer has been terminated so that it is no longer capable of being accepted; and
- advising on when a contract might be void for uncertainty or otherwise because the parties have not reached agreement on all material terms.

1.1 Introduction

Consumers and businesses enter into contracts on a regular basis. For example, manufacturers need to buy raw materials to make their products; then they sell those products to wholesalers and/or retailers who then ultimately sell them to us as consumers. Whilst we ourselves may not always think about the legal consequences of what we are doing until something goes wrong (eg the holiday we booked turns out to be a disaster), many businesses employ a dedicated contracts manager.

When something does go wrong (eg goods supplied are defective) the first thing to consider is whether there was a contract and, if so, on what terms. We will be looking at terms of a contract in **Part 2**, **Chapters 6** and **7**. In **Part 1** we shall simply be focusing on what constitutes a binding contract in the first place.

In order for parties to reach an agreement, one party must make an offer (ie a definite promise to be bound by specified terms) that is accepted by the other. The person who makes the offer is called the offeror and the person to whom the offer is made is called the offeree. We begin by looking at what is deemed to be an 'offer' in the eyes of the law.

1.2 Offers and invitations to treat

An offer has been defined as 'an expression of willingness to contract on certain terms, made with the intention that it shall become binding as soon as it is accepted by the person to whom it is addressed' (Treitel, *The Law of Contract*, 14th edn (2015), p 10).

An 'expression' may take many different forms eg a letter, newspaper advertisement, email, text message and even conduct, as long as it communicates the basis on which the offeror is prepared to contract.

The 'intention' referred to in the definition does not necessarily mean the offeror's actual intention. The courts adopt what is primarily an 'objective' approach to deciding whether there was agreement between the parties. Clearly, they cannot discover as a matter of fact what was going on in the minds of the parties at the time of the alleged agreement. Nor are they prepared simply to accept what the parties themselves say was their intention at that time (which would be a 'subjective' approach). Instead, the courts look at what was said and done between the parties, from the point of view of a 'reasonable person', and try to decide what a reasonable person would have thought was going on.

✪ Example

Faheem had been advised by a motorcycle dealer to ask at least £6,000 for his motorcycle. Faheem texted John offering to sell it to him for £5,000. On reading the text message John immediately telephoned Faheem and agreed to pay £5,000 for the motorcycle. Faheem told him that he would not accept less than £6,000 for the motorcycle. He said he was sorry if the price stated in the text message was not £6,000, but that it must have been an error, which he had not noticed.

Although Faheem in fact intended to sell the motorcycle for £6,000, the price mentioned in his text message was £5,000. Assuming that this communication was the only one between the parties regarding the price, a reasonable person would assume that £5,000 was the intended asking price. Also, as far as we can determine, John believed that Faheem was making an offer to sell the motorcycle for £5,000. Faheem would be bound to sell the motorcycle to John for £5,000.

Finally, Treitel's definition of an offer refers to 'the person to whom it is addressed'. This may be one person, a class of persons or even the whole world. (You will see an example of an offer made to the public in **1.2.2** below.) The point is that you can only accept an offer that was addressed to you.

An offer needs to be distinguished from an invitation to treat. Imagine I said to you: 'I am thinking of selling my car. I have been told that £7,000 would be a realistic asking price. Would you be interested in buying it?' This would not amount to an offer as I have only said that I am 'thinking' of selling my car, and the price is only a potential asking price. I have not committed myself to selling you the car at a specific price. The legal terminology for such preliminary statements is 'invitation to treat'. The statements are simply inviting negotiation and so the buyer could not by agreeing to pay £7,000 for the car thereby create a binding contract. Compare this invitation to treat with an offer eg 'I *will* sell you my car for £7,000'.

1.2.1 Goods on display

So what about goods on display eg on the shelves in a supermarket? Are they an offer or an invitation to treat? To decide this, it might be easier for you to work backwards and think where a contract is actually concluded in a supermarket. It is at the checkout. You offer to buy the goods and it is up to the cashier to decide whether, or not, to accept that offer. So goods on display are simply an invitation to treat ie an invitation to select the goods and put them in your trolley. If you later change your mind and decide you do not want the goods then you can put them back without obligation.

1.2.2 Advertisements

Where goods or services are advertised (eg in a newspaper, a television commercial or on a website) this is generally regarded as being an invitation to treat. Why? Because if such advertisements were offers, it would mean that anyone asking for the advertised goods would be accepting and that would be a problem if the advertiser had run out of stock.

What about an advert of a reward? Traditionally adverts of reward have been treated as offers; namely definite promises to pay the reward if the specified condition (eg supply of information) is satisfied. There is a policy reason behind this approach. Treating advertisements of a reward as offers means that the money has to be paid once the offer is accepted eg by the supply of the information. No negotiation is involved. This should encourage people who have information to come forward.

Advertisements of reward, then, are offers, but other types of advertisement will usually be invitations to treat. However, if there are special circumstances that show an intention to be bound, an advert may amount to an offer – an offer of a unilateral contract.

Most contracts are bilateral (ie a promise in return for a promise) but with unilateral contracts only one party is making a promise (eg a promise to pay a reward); hence why they are said to be unilateral. No one is bound to do the specified act. This is why unilateral contracts are sometimes referred to as 'If' contracts. '*If* you do X, I promise to do Y.'

The distinction between unilateral and bilateral contracts is particularly important in relation to 'acceptance' and 'consideration' (which we will cover in **1.3** below and **Chapter 3** respectively).

 The formation of a unilateral contract can be demonstrated in the famous case of Carlill v Carbolic Smoke Ball Company *[1893] 1 QB 256 (CA).*

*In order to guarantee the effectiveness of the smoke ball remedy, the company offered a reward of £100 to anyone who used the remedy and contracted flu. They also confirmed that they had deposited £1,000 in a bank account ready to make any payments under their promise, showing great confidence in the smoke ball and further tempting customers to buy one (see **Figure 1.1**).*

Figure 1.1 Carbolic Smoke Ball offer

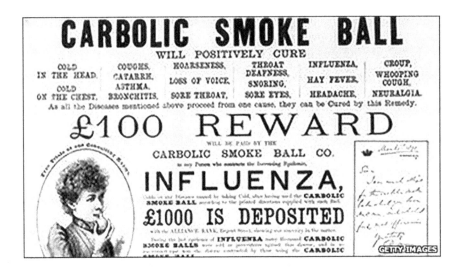

Once aware of the offer, Mrs Carlill accepted it when she purchased the smoke ball; she completed the prescribed course and then contracted flu. She sued for the £100 and the court held that the company's promise to pay £100 was an offer of a unilateral contract ie a promise in return for the specified act that Mrs Carlill had performed.

1.2.3 Auctions and tenders

1.2.3.1 Auctions

If you attend an auction at what point do you think a sale is concluded? When is an offer accepted? It is when the auctioneer's gavel goes down; that is the acceptance of the last bid, which was the offer (Sale of Goods Act (SGA) 1979, s 57(2)). The auctioneer inviting bids is simply an invitation to treat.

Owners of household items being sold at an auction are generally prepared to accept whatever price someone is prepared to bid for them. But what about expensive assets such as houses? The owner and auctioneer will generally agree in advance a minimum price below which the auctioneer will not sell the property. Such a price is called a 'reserve price'. Potential bidders will be made aware there is a reserve price; they just will not know what it is. What they do know, though, is that if the bidding does not reach the reserve price the property will be withdrawn from the sale.

Auctions of lots that do not have a reserve price may be advertised as being 'without reserve'. The legal significance of this is highlighted by the decision in *Barry v Davies* [2000] 1 WLR 1962.

In Barry v Davies *two machines being sold at an auction were advertised by the auctioneer as being 'sold without reserve'; in other words they would be sold to whoever made the highest bid (however much that might be). Mr Barry made the highest bid for the machines but the auctioneer did not accept it as he knew he could get a much higher price for them elsewhere. Mr Barry successfully sued the auctioneer for breach of contract; more specifically for breach of a unilateral contract. Why unilateral? Only one party had made a promise, namely the auctioneer. He had promised to sell the machines to whoever might make the highest bid. Why would it have been pointless Mr Barry suing the owner of the machines? The auctioneer had not accepted his bid and so there was no contract of sale with the owner.*

The measure of Mr Barry's damages was the difference between the amount of his bid (£400) and the total value of the machines (£28,000) ie £27,600. That sum represented his loss of expectation: he had expected to buy the machines for £400 but it would cost Mr Barry another £27,600 to buy similar machines elsewhere. The amount the auctioneer sold the machines for elsewhere was irrelevant. We will consider damages in detail in **Chapter 8**.

1.2.3.2 Tenders

It is not uncommon for services to be contracted out by businesses. For example, a manufacturing company may decide to outsource its cleaning services and invite a number of companies to submit tenders for the work. Does it have to accept any particular one of them? Generally no, because the invitation was simply an invitation to treat and the tenders will each have been offers to do the work. But what if the company had specifically promised to accept the lowest tender, or at least impliedly promised to consider all conforming tenders? Then what we have is an offer of a unilateral contract and if the company does not comply with its promise (to, say, accept the lowest tender) it will be liable for breach of contract.

 In Blackpool & Fylde Aero Club Ltd v Blackpool Borough Council [1990] 1 WLR 1195 (CA) the Aero Club had been granted a number of concessions to operate pleasure flights from Blackpool airport. When the last concession was nearing expiry, the council sent invitations to tender to the claimant and six other interested parties. The invitation said that the tenders had to be received not later than noon on 17 March 1983. The Aero Club posted its tender in the Town Hall letter box at 11am on 17 March. The letter box was supposed to be emptied at noon each day, but due to an oversight was not emptied at noon on 17 March. Consequently, the claimant's tender was recorded as late and not considered. The Aero Club successfully sued for breach of an implied promise that a tender, returned on time, would at least be considered. The council was in breach of an implied unilateral contract to consider any conforming tenders and so was liable to the Aero Club for loss of opportunity (see **Chapter 8**).

1.3 Acceptance

1.3.1 Definition

So far we have considered 'offer', which is the first constituent of agreement. An offer must be in a form whereby a simple assent to it is enough to lead to agreement. In many cases, therefore, it is enough if the person to whom the offer is made simply says 'Yes, I agree'. In some situations, however, it may be more difficult to decide precisely if, and when, a matching offer and acceptance have been made.

Acceptance has been defined as an unqualified expression of assent to the terms of an offer. So to be acceptance there must be:

(a) an expression of assent,

(b) which is 'unqualified'.

1.3.2 Communication of acceptance

The need for an 'expression of assent' means that, generally speaking, acceptance must be communicated and it must be communicated by the offeree or their authorised agent. This may be by words or conduct. A nod or a wink can say a lot. Acceptance of an offer of a unilateral contract will always be conduct of some sort.

So what about silence? Can that ever amount to acceptance? If coupled with conduct that clearly signifies acceptance when viewed objectively, then the answer is 'yes'. However, as a general rule an offeror cannot bind the other party to a contract by silence per se.

The need for the expression to be 'unqualified' means that a conditional response cannot amount to acceptance and create a contract. The legal terminology for a conditional response (such as 'I agree to buy your car, but can only afford to pay you half the price now and the rest next week') is a counter-offer. The offeree has imposed a condition on their acceptance. A counter-offer effectively destroys the original offer and represents a new offer that the other party is free to accept or reject.

Businesses generally want to contract on their own standard terms and conditions (Ts & Cs) rather than those of the other party. In an attempt to achieve this they will attach their Ts & Cs to any document they submit to the other side (whether that be a quotation or, say, an order form). A so-called battle of the forms may result, with both sides passing their own Ts & Cs to the other side for agreement. These can be seen as counter-offer after counter-offer. The parties battle it out and the prize is having your own terms prevail. In other words, the last shot wins.

 A case that illustrates this is Butler Machine Tool v Ex-Cell-O Corp *[1979] 1 WLR 401. The sellers sent a quotation (offer) for the supply of machines to the buyer. This offer was subject to a price variation clause. The buyers purported to accept on the buyer's Ts & Cs (which did not include a price variation clause). At the end of the order was a tear-off acknowledgement of order form that said, 'We accept your order on the Ts & Cs stated therein'. The sellers returned the tear-off slip and in so doing effectively accepted the buyer's 'last shot'.*

The decision in Butler Machine Tool Co Ltd v Ex-Cell-O Corporation (England) Ltd, *however, did little to resolve a true 'battle of the forms', such as might have arisen if there had been no acknowledgement slip, but simply an exchange of incompatible terms, followed by the delivery of the machine. In such a situation, delivery of the machine might be regarded as acceptance by conduct of the last set of standard terms to be proffered.*

1.3.3 Acceptance by post

As stated above, the general rule is that acceptance must be communicated but when post is chosen as the mode of acceptance there is bound to be a delay between the letter of acceptance being sent and it actually being received and read. So when does the law deem a letter of acceptance to be effective? By virtue of what has become known as the 'postal rule' a letter of acceptance will be effective when posted even if the letter is lost in the post. For the postal rule to apply, though, the following conditions must be satisfied:

(a) it was reasonable in all the circumstances to use the post;

(b) the letter was properly addressed, stamped and posted; and

(c) the postal rule had not been excluded by the offeror.

The rule would be excluded if, for example, the offeror had stipulated or otherwise implied that they needed to be notified in writing or 'told' of any acceptance. In that case, although sending a letter of acceptance might be reasonable it would only be effective if, and when, received.

 In the case of Holwell Securities Ltd v Hughes *[1974] 1 WLR 155 (CA) the defendant granted the claimant an option to buy a house expressed as being 'exercisable by notice in writing to [the defendant]'. The claimant wrote to the defendant purporting to exercise the option but the letter never arrived. If the postal rule applied there would have been a binding contract at the time of posting (irrespective of the fact the notice did not arrive); whereas if the postal rule did not apply, there would be no contract, as acceptance had not been communicated.*

Agreement

Thinking back to the limitations on the postal rule, the post was clearly a reasonable method of acceptance, as notice had to be in writing and there was no urgency. But even assuming that the notice had been properly addressed and posted etc, the offer said 'notice in writing to [the defendant]' and the court held that, by using the word 'notice', the offeror had impliedly excluded the postal rule. So whilst it might have been appropriate to accept by post, the acceptance actually had to arrive with the defendant to be effective. The postal rule did not apply. **Figure 1.2** *summarises the position.*

Figure 1.2 Acceptance by post

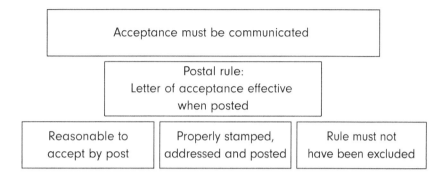

1.4 Termination of offers

An offer cannot be accepted once it has been terminated. An offer may be terminated in the following ways (also in **Figure 1.3**):

(a) Rejection by the offeree

Figure 1.3 Termination of offers

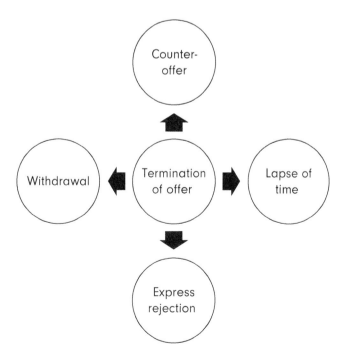

9

(b) Revocation (ie withdrawal) of the offer by the offeror

(c) Lapse of time

1.4.1 Rejection

An offer may be rejected by the offeree either expressly or impliedly. It will be rejected by implication if the offeree makes a counter-offer (see **1.3.2** above).

1.4.2 Revocation

Generally an offer may be revoked (withdrawn) any time before acceptance even if the offeror promised to keep the offer open for a certain period of time. The only exception to that is if the offeree gave something in return for the promise to keep the offer open (eg if the offeree paid the offeror £1 for the privilege of having a specific period of time within which to accept) then the offer would have to be kept open for the agreed time.

 *In Mountford v Scott [1975] 1 All ER 198, the claimant paid £1 for the option to buy V's house for £10,000. The option was exercisable within six months. V purported to revoke the offer. The claimant subsequently sought to exercise the option. The court held that the offer was irrevocable as the claimant had paid for the option (albeit a nominal amount). In paying £1, the claimant had given consideration for the offeror's promise to leave the offer open for six months. We shall look at consideration in **Chapter 3**.*

So the general rule is that an offer can be revoked any time before acceptance but in relation to offers of unilateral contracts when does acceptance take place? Is it when the promisee starts to perform the required act, or only when they complete it?

 Example

Someone offers to pay you £100 if you walk from London to York. Do you accept this offer when you first embark on the walk, or when you actually arrive at York? The general view is that with unilateral contracts no obligations arise until the specified act is completed; in other words, acceptance only occurs when performance is complete. That being so, it would mean that the offer of £100 could be withdrawn at any time before you complete your walk to York. You could be just five miles away from York when you are told that the offer no longer stands and you would have no redress. It would be grossly unfair, and accordingly there are a number of judicial authorities that suggest partial performance of a unilateral contract is sufficient to prevent revocation by the offeror.

It has been suggested that there are two offers in this situation. In addition to the express offer, there is an implied promise not to revoke if the specified act is started within a reasonable time. The acceptance and consideration for the implied promise is the commencement of the act.

Revocation, however, must be communicated to the offeree in order to be effective. Consider notice of revocation sent by email. When do you think that would be effectively communicated? When it was sent, when it was actually read or when it should have been read? In relation to electronic communications sent to a business the rule appears to be that revocation will be effective when it should have been read.

 Authority for this is The Brimnes *[1975] QB 929. On the facts a shipowner had the right to withdraw a ship by a given day if the hire fee was not paid on time; notice of withdrawal of the ship was sent by telex, and received during office hours at 5.45pm; but the notice was not read until the next morning (which would have been too late to give the notice).*

The Court of Appeal held that it was communicated when it was received, if it was communicated by such means that it would in the normal course of business come to the

attention of the person on its arrival, but for their failure to act in a normal business-like manner.

What about an offer made to the public at large as in *Carlill v Carbolic Smoke Ball Co*? How can the offeror possibly know who has seen the offer and therefore tell them that it has been withdrawn? The best the offeror can do in the circumstances is publish a notice of revocation in the same place as the offer and with the same prominence and in an American case, which is persuasive, this was held to be effective.

Notice of revocation can be given either by the offeror or a reliable third party (ie someone objectively considered to be reliable). Note this is different to communication of acceptance in the following respects:

- acceptance must be communicated by the offeree or an authorised agent; and
- the postal rule does not apply to notices of revocation.

1.4.3 Lapse of time

An offer will lapse after a specified time, or otherwise after a reasonable time. What would be a reasonable time will depend on all the circumstances, eg a reasonable time within which to accept an offer to buy perishable goods will be significantly less than in the case of an offer to sell non-perishables.

1.5 Certainty and completeness

So far we have considered 'agreement' in its simplest form, ie an offer that has been accepted. But often in real life it is not that straightforward, eg, if commercial parties have been negotiating terms over a considerable period of time it may be difficult to assess if, and when, they reached agreement on all the material terms of the deal.

Whether, or not, parties have reached complete agreement in relation to the material terms of the deal is generally judged objectively, but the facts have to be judged in context, eg:

(a) whether the parties are in the same trade;

(b) trade usage;

(c) whether the arrangement has been acted on for any length of time; and

(d) whether there is an objective mechanism for resolving any uncertainty such as an arbitration clause.

Examples

*(a) You go to a car dealership and say you are interested in buying a particular car priced at £10,500. You agree to buy it on 'hire purchase terms'. In the absence of any other details of the hire purchase agreement (eg duration, number and amount of repayments) it would be too vague to be a contract (*Scammell v Ouston *[1941] AC 251 (HL)).*

(b) An agreement to buy 'timber of fair specification'. This may seem vague but the court held there was a binding contract on the particular facts of a case. The parties had dealt with each other in the past; they were well acquainted with the timber trade; and the contract had been partly performed. In other words, as far as the parties themselves were concerned there was no uncertainty.

(c) An agreement between a petrol company and filling station to supply petrol at the market price prevailing at the date of delivery. Although the exact price has not been

Contract

agreed, if the agreement provides a mechanism by which the uncertainty can be resolved there would be a binding contract.

(d) *A 'provisional agreement' is drawn up and is to operate until a fully legalised agreement drawn up by a solicitor and embodying the conditions of the provisional agreement is signed. The fact that a formalised agreement has yet to be drawn up is irrelevant. Generally contracts do not have to be in any particular form, and clearly the parties are in agreement and so there would be a contract.*

Summary

- For a contract there must be agreement (comprising an offer that has been accepted), intention to create legal relations and consideration (see **Figure 1.4**).
- Most contracts are bilateral, ie a promise in return for a promise. A unilateral contract is a promise in return for an act.
- As far as agreement is concerned an offer must have been accepted and all material terms must have been agreed.
- An offer must be distinguished from an invitation to treat, which cannot be accepted.
- An offer cannot be accepted once it has been terminated, eg by rejection, revocation or lapse of time. Revocation must be communicated.
- Acceptance must be unconditional and communicated by words or conduct; but, if the postal rule applies, a letter of acceptance will be binding when it is posted.

Figure 1.4 Requirements for formation of a contract

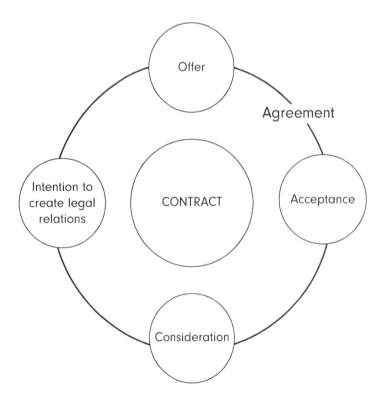

Sample questions

Question 1

A client wanted a skip to take away rubbish and so contacted a skip hire company. The company posted a quotation for £90 and said that if the client wanted to accept the company needed to know by Friday 19 April.

On Tuesday 16 April the client posted a letter accepting the quotation and asking when would be the earliest the company could supply a skip. By 22 April the client had not heard back from the company. The client rang the company. It said it had not received the letter and had no skips available for hire now or in the near future.

If the client sued the company for breach of contract, which of the following best describes the most likely outcome?

- A The company would be liable for breach because a contract was formed when the client posted the letter on 16 April.
- B The company would not be liable for breach of contract because the client's letter on 16 April amounted to a counter-offer.
- C The company would not be liable for breach of contract as it had no more skips available.
- D The company would be liable for breach of contract as the client accepted its offer when the client rang on 22 April.
- E The company would not be liable for breach of contract as the postal rule would not apply.

Answer

The correct answer is E.

An offer was made by the company to hire out the skip for £90. The client purported to accept on Tuesday 16 April. The letter was not a counter-offer as the client was only asking a question and not imposing a condition, so B is wrong. Acceptance must be communicated. On that basis the client has no contract with the company, because by the time the client actually contacted the company (ie on 22 April) its offer had lapsed (19 April), so D is wrong.

There will only be a contract if the postal rule applied. Under the postal rule a letter of acceptance is binding as soon as it is posted. For the rule to apply the post must have been a reasonable means of communication. On the facts it may have been reasonable to reply by post on 16 April as the offer did not lapse until 19 April and also the quote had been sent by post. Query though whether the letter was sent first or second class and at what time (eg was it posted after the last postal collection on 16 April?).

In any event the postal rule will only apply where a letter was properly addressed and posted etc. Query here why the client's letter was lost in the post, eg had it been properly addressed? Also the postal rule may have been impliedly excluded as the company said it needed to 'know' by 19 April. Only in the unlikely event of the postal rule applying would there be a contract. This is why A is wrong.

C is wrong because even if the company had no more skips it could be in breach and liable to pay damages.

Question 2

A client attended an auction. When it came to the lot comprising Victorian garden ornaments, the auctioneer said they had been valued at £300 and would be sold that day whatever price they fetched. He invited bids of £100, then £80. When nobody responded, the auctioneer asked how much anyone would be prepared to pay for the ornaments and the client bid £20. No further bids were made but the auctioneer withdrew the ornaments from the sale. He later sold them privately for £150.

Which of the following statements best sums up the legal position of the client?

A   The client could sue the owner of the ornaments for breach of a contract.

B   The client could sue the auctioneer for breach of contract and the measure of damages would be £130.

C   The client could sue the auctioneer for breach of a unilateral contract.

D   The client would not have an action for breach of contract as the bid was far too low.

E   The client could sue the auctioneer for breach of a bilateral contract and the measure of damages would be £280.

Answer

The correct statement is C.

Normally at an auction the bids are the offers and the fall of the auctioneer's hammer is the acceptance (SGA 1979, s 57). Therefore, the client had no contract to buy the ornaments from the seller as the auctioneer did not accept the bid. Hence A is wrong.

Here the auctioneer made an offer of a unilateral contract when he said that the ornaments would 'be sold that day whatever price they fetched'. This is why E is wrong. He was promising to sell to whoever made the highest bid (*Barry v Davies*) but he did not then sell to the highest bidder so he was in breach of contract. The amount of the bid is irrelevant and that is why D is wrong.

The auctioneer will be liable in damages to the client for £280, ie the difference between the value of the ornaments (£300) and the amount of the client's bid (£20), so B is wrong.

Question 3

At 9am a car dealer emailed a client offering to sell her a vintage car for £60,000. The client received the email shortly afterwards and emailed an acceptance of the offer at 12.55pm. The client knew that the car dealership closes for lunch each day between 1pm and 2pm. After lunch the car dealer did not check his email account. At 2.30pm the car dealer received an offer for £62,000 for the vintage car, which he accepted. At 4pm the client phoned the car dealer to enquire about the car and was told the car was no longer for sale. The client has been reliably informed it will cost £65,000 to buy a similar car elsewhere.

Which of the following statements best sums up the legal position of the client?

A   The client has a contract with the dealer to buy the car and can sue the dealer for £2,000 representing the profit the dealer made on selling the car elsewhere.

B   The dealer revoked his offer before acceptance was communicated and so there would be no contract of sale with the client.

C   The client's acceptance would be deemed communicated before 2.30pm and so the dealer would be liable to pay the client damages of £5,000.

D   By virtue of the postal rule, acceptance was communicated at 12.55pm and so the dealer would be liable to the client for breach.

E   When the dealer sold the car elsewhere he effectively revoked the offer to the client and so would not be liable for breach.

Answer

The correct answer is C. Acceptance would be deemed communicated when it would be reasonable for the client to expect it to be read. With businesses it is reasonable to expect communications to be read during normal office hours (so here not between 1pm and 2pm but certainly before 2.30pm). Also the aim of contractual damages is to compensate the innocent party for loss of bargain. Here it will cost the client an extra £5,000 to buy a similar car elsewhere. This is why A is wrong.

B is wrong as it is likely acceptance would be deemed communicated before the offer was revoked at 4pm.

D is wrong as the postal rule only applies to letters of acceptance.

E is wrong as revocation must be communicated (by the offeror or a reliable third party).

2 Intention to Create Legal Relations

2.1	Introduction	18
2.2	Commercial agreements	18
2.3	Domestic agreements	19

SQE1 syllabus

This chapter will enable you to achieve the SQE1 assessment specification in relation to functioning legal knowledge of the intention to create legal relations, which is one of the three essential elements of a binding contract. The other two elements needed for a contract are agreement (comprising an offer that has been accepted, which we looked at in **Chapter 1**) and consideration (which is covered in **Chapter 3**).

Note that, for SQE1, candidates are not usually required to recall specific case names or cite statutory or regulatory authorities. Cases are provided for illustrative purposes only.

Learning outcomes

By the end of this chapter you will be able to apply relevant core legal principles and rules appropriately and effectively, at the level of a competent newly qualified solicitor in practice, to realistic client-based and ethical problems and situations in the following areas:

- establishing whether intention to create legal relations is present in a commercial context; and
- advising on whether, or not, intention to create legal relations is present in a domestic agreement.

2.1 Introduction

People reach all sorts of agreement with one another – some are obviously meant to be legally binding, eg if you paid for an OLED 4K Ultra HD TV and it did not arrive, you would, ultimately, expect to end up in court. But some agreements are not meant to be legally binding, eg you agree to mow the lawn if your partner washes the dishes.

Why the difference? The law takes the view that whether an agreement is to be legally binding depends on whether the parties had an intention to create legal relations. When you buy an expensive TV, you almost certainly do have an intention to create legal relations – perhaps taking a retailer to court is a last resort, but it is still an option. On the other hand, mowing the lawn if your partner washes the dishes is not an agreement you would have meant to have legal consequences. That would not be because you had not struck a deal: it is just that you will sort out your differences in private rather than in the courtroom.

Of course, things are only likely to get tricky when one party says the agreement *was* meant to be legally binding, and the other says it was not. Then, the court will have to decide whether the agreement was intended to be legally binding before it will enforce it.

To help decide, the law operates on the basis of rebuttable presumptions, which differ according to whether the agreement is to be regarded as 'commercial' or 'domestic'. With commercial agreements there is a very strong presumption that the parties intended their agreement to have legal consequences; whereas with domestic agreements (ie agreements reached between family members or friends) the presumption is that the parties did not intend to create legal relations. Both presumptions may be rebutted, ie they will apply unless the facts show otherwise (see **Figure 2.1**).

Figure 2.1 Intention to create legal relations

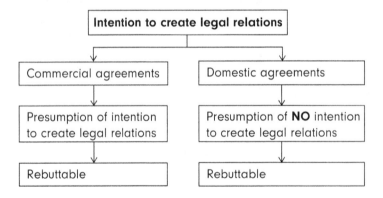

2.2 Commercial agreements

When we talk about commercial agreements we do not just mean agreements between businesses. We also mean agreements between individuals and businesses, eg when you go shopping or buy something over the internet. We even mean agreements between individuals not in business, eg if you bought a second-hand bicycle out of the newspaper.

In the case of commercial agreements, the law presumes that the agreement is intended to be legally binding even if the subject matter of the transaction is trivial. In other words, there is a very strong presumption of intention to create legal relations in a commercial context.

> *This is demonstrated by the case of* Esso Petroleum v Commissioners of Customs and Excise *[1976] 1 WLR 1. In the 1970s, Esso ran a sales promotion offering a 'free' World Cup coin for every four gallons of fuel purchased. The coins clearly had very little intrinsic*

value and if Esso ran out of coins, disappointed motorists were highly unlikely to take Esso to court. Nevertheless, the House of Lords held that the parties did intend to create legal relations. Whilst the coins in themselves might have been of minimal value, the incentive to soccer enthusiasts to collect all 30 coins was strong; and to that extent the offer of the coins was of significant economic value to Esso.

So in a commercial context there is a very strong presumption the parties intended their agreement to have legal consequences. Indeed, there have been very few cases involving commercial agreements where the presumption of intention to create legal relations has been successfully rebutted. A clear, express statement that the agreement is not meant to be legally binding (eg a statement to the effect the agreement is 'binding in honour only') would work, but not much short of that.

2.3 Domestic agreements

When we talk about domestic agreements, we mean those where the parties are family members, close friends or the like.

Where an agreement is domestic, the law presumes that the agreement is not intended to be legally binding unless the facts show otherwise. So, with domestic agreements, there is a presumption of no intention to create legal relations but if the facts *do* show otherwise, then the presumption is rebutted. The law in this area arises from cases where one party says that the evidence has rebutted the particular presumption, but the other party says it has not.

 Examples

Table 2.1 contains some examples of agreements between family members or friends and the sort of matters the court will take into account in deciding whether their agreement was intended to be legally binding.

Table 2.1   Intention to create legal relations in domestic agreements

Parties	Relevant fact	Intention?
Husband and wife	Solicitors are settling the financial terms of their divorce	Yes. The parties are dealing at arm's length. Solicitors are involved and any agreement will be formalised.
Two friends	Reach agreement on how they will contribute to a joint business venture	Yes. A lot of money would be at stake.
A brother and sister	Expressly agree that their agreement will be legally binding	Yes. The presumption would be rebutted as the parties have reached express agreement.
Two cousins	One sells their house to the other	Yes. The relationship is not particularly close but the agreement is about an asset of considerable worth and will have been formalised.
Parent and child	They agree what the child must do in order to get their weekly financial allowance of £10	No. The relationship is very close and the sum involved is nominal.

Contract

Summary

- In a commercial context there is a very strong presumption that the parties intend to create legal relations. Clear words are needed to rebut this presumption.
- Between family and friends there is a rebuttable presumption that they do not intend their agreement to have legal consequences.

Sample question

Question 1

Which of the following statements best sums up legal principles that govern intentions to create legal relations?

A   With commercial agreements there is a non-rebuttable presumption of intention to create legal relations; whereas with domestic agreements there is no intention to create legal relations.

B   With domestic agreements there is a strong presumption of no intention to create legal relations that is difficult to rebut unless very clear words are used.

C   With all agreements involving individuals the presumption is that they did not intend to create legal relations; whereas in business-to-business contracts there is a very strong presumption the parties intended legal relations.

D   In a commercial context there is a strong presumption that the parties intended legal relations but it may be rebutted if the agreement is stated to be 'binding in honour only'.

E   With domestic agreements it is irrebuttably presumed the parties did not intend legal consequences.

Answer

The correct statement is D.

Commercial agreements do not just cover business-to-business contracts; they cover all agreements that are not made between family and friends. This is why C is wrong. Both presumptions are rebuttable hence why A and E are wrong. The commercial presumption is very strong and difficult to rebut unless clear words are used. The presumption in relation to domestic agreements may be rebutted by a number of factors including how close is the parties' relationship and the amount of money at stake – hence why B is wrong.

3 Consideration

3.1	Identifying consideration	22
3.2	Contractual variations	24
3.3	Alteration promises to pay more	24
3.4	Alteration promises to accept less	26

SQE1 syllabus

This chapter will enable you to achieve the SQE1 assessment specification in relation to functioning legal knowledge of the core principles of consideration in the context of contract formation and variation. Consideration is one of the three essential elements for a contract and any contractual variation. The other two elements needed are agreement (**Chapter 1**) and intention to create legal relations (**Chapter 2**).

Note that, for SQE1, candidates are not usually required to recall specific case names or cite statutory or regulatory authorities. Cases are provided for illustrative purposes only.

Learning outcomes

By the end of this chapter you will be able to apply relevant core legal principles and rules appropriately and effectively, at the level of a competent newly qualified solicitor in practice, to realistic client-based and ethical problems and situations in the following areas:

- identifying consideration in relation to the formation and variation of contracts;
- alteration promises to pay more; and
- alteration promises to accept less.

3.1 Identifying consideration

The need for consideration is the idea that, in order to be able to hold the other party to a promise, you must have agreed to provide 'something in return' for that promise: it is this 'something in return' that lawyers call 'consideration'.

The 'something in return' may be a promise (called executory consideration) or an act (executed consideration). Bilateral contracts by their nature involve an exchange of promises; whereas a unilateral contract comprises a promise in return for an act (**Chapter 1**).

So in order to sue for breach of a promise, a party must be able to show they gave consideration for that promise.

 Example

I agree to buy a laptop off you for £500. I can hold you to the deal because I have agreed to pay for it. I have 'provided consideration' for your promise to sell me the laptop. The consideration would be my promise to pay £500 for it: that is a benefit to you and a detriment to me.

Equally, you could hold me to the deal: you agreed to hand over the laptop in return for getting my £500. That is a detriment to you and a corresponding benefit to me. Indeed, one of the well-established definitions of consideration is 'benefit OR detriment'. It need not be both; although as you have just seen, there will often be both benefit and detriment.

There are two other key issues. One of them, contract lawyers call 'adequacy of consideration'; the other, they call 'sufficiency of consideration'. They sound similar, but lawyers mean different things by them.

3.1.1 Consideration need not be adequate

Think of 'adequacy' as concerned with the *amount* or *value* of the 'something in return'. The law is not concerned whether what is provided in return is of the same value as the promise for which it is given. It simply has to have some value. For example, payment of £1 would be good consideration for an Aston Martin car. £1 would be sufficient because it is of some value. The fact that it is not equivalent in value to the car (ie not adequate consideration) does not matter. Contracts are voluntarily entered into, and the law takes the view that, by and large, people should be free to strike the deals they want.

The fact that consideration must have some value has traditionally been interpreted to mean that it must have some economic value, albeit nominal. Nowadays, however, the need for 'economic value' does not seem to be a strict one.

3.1.2 Consideration must be sufficient

Sufficiency is concerned not with the amount of the consideration, but with the sort of thing it is.

What is provided in return must be the sort of thing the law regards as being appropriate subject matter for a bargain. As far as the formation of a contract is concerned, it is very clear in most cases. Such things as money, goods and services are provided in exchange for the other party's commitment. These are definitely the right sort of thing – they are at the heart of what contracts are all about.

In fact, there are very few cases where the law has not regarded consideration as the right 'sort' of thing – one case was where a promise was made 'in consideration of natural love and affection'; another where what was promised in exchange was 'to stop complaining about being disinherited'. The law has not regarded such things as the proper subject matter of true 'exchanges'.

But what about a promise to stop swearing, gambling, drinking alcohol and smoking tobacco? Do you think that would be appropriate subject matter for a bargain? Where is the detriment in promising not to smoke tobacco? Smoking tobacco is bad for one's health and so refraining from doing so would actually benefit the promisor. What if the promisor had never smoked, gambled, sworn or drank alcohol and had no intention of doing so? Where would the benefit or detriment be then? These were all questions considered by an American court. People have a right to swear, drink alcohol etc and as a matter of public policy should be positively encouraged not to do so: hence, a promise to refrain from doing them was held to be sufficient consideration.

Do not be surprised; public policy quite often plays a significant part in the decision making of our courts. For example, it no doubt explains why performance of a public duty is not regarded as sufficient or good consideration, whereas exceeding a public duty is regarded as sufficient consideration for a promise.

⭐ Examples

You are summoned to appear as a witness in a criminal trial. The defendant promises to pay you £50 for doing so but afterwards refuses to pay. You could not enforce the promise because you were legally obliged to give evidence and so had not given consideration.

If you had exceeded a legal (public) duty, though, that would have been different; that would have been consideration.

3.1.3 Past consideration

The need for an exchange and something given in return explains why performance of a gratuitous act or promise is not deemed to be consideration for a later promise of payment. What was done or promised was not done or promised in return for anything at all. It had been gratuitous.

⭐ Example

As a favour, Helen looks after Carl's cat while Carl is on holiday. When Carl returns he promises to give Helen £30. Helen would not be able to enforce that promise because she did not look after Carl's cat in return for payment. Carl promised £30 afterwards. She had looked after the cat purely and simply as a favour.

From this we get the phrase 'past consideration is not good consideration'; although, like with most general principles in contract law, it is not an absolute rule and there is an exception provided the following conditions are satisfied:

(a) the past act/promise was done at the promisor's request;

(b) there was a mutual understanding between the parties that the act/promise would be compensated for in some way; and

(c) had the promise been made in advance it would have been legally enforceable. This last condition often hinges on whether, or not, there would have been the necessary intention to create legal relations (see **Chapter 2**).

⭕ *A case in which all the above conditions were satisfied was* Re Casey's Patents *[1892] 1 Ch 669. A manager was asked to promote a particular invention for the owner of the patent rights for a two-year period. Afterwards the owners promised him a share in those rights in consideration for what he had done. It was alleged that the promise was unenforceable as being supported only by past consideration. In finding the promise to be enforceable the court said there was an implied promise to pay in the circumstances and that the manager must always have assumed that he would be rewarded in some way for what he had done. The later promise simply crystallised what he would get.*

3.1.4 Consideration – summary

Figure 3.1 summarises the key points we have considered. In the big scheme of things, the requirement for consideration rarely causes a problem at the point of formation of a contract. The law relating to sufficiency of consideration is of greater consequence in relation to the later variation of contracts.

Figure 3.1 Consideration requirements

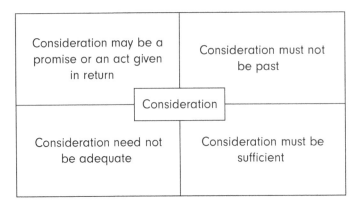

3.2 Contractual variations

When parties enter into a long term contract they should anticipate that circumstances may change and that at some future date one or both parties may wish to vary the contract. This might be for any number of reasons, for example an economic recession, an increase in the value of raw materials, or because of a change in the exchange rate.

So what then must parties do if they wish to vary a contract and ensure that the variation will be binding? Well just as you need agreement, consideration and intention to create legal relations to form a contract you need the same three things in order to make a contractual variation binding. Often the stumbling block is consideration. The parties have agreed the change and intend it to be legally binding but, for some reason or another, the variation is one-sided. Only one of the parties is suffering a detriment, or otherwise conferring a benefit on the other party.

⭐ *Example*

An employer has genuine cause for concern that a contractor may not be able to finish a job on the agreed completion date and so promises them extra money if they will do so. What, if anything, have they given in return for the promise of the extra money? They have simply performed an existing contractual duty owed to the employer. Where is the detriment in that to the contractor, or the benefit to the employer? It is these so-called 'upward' variations that we are going to focus on next.

3.3 Alteration promises to pay more

Not surprisingly, the general rule is that simply performing an existing contractual duty owed to the other party will not be consideration in exchange for a promise by the other party to pay more money.

But what if a party exceeds a contractual obligation owed to the other party in return for a promise of extra money? Then there is clearly a detriment to the promisee and a benefit to the promisor; so it *will* be consideration for the promise of the extra cash.

⭐ Example

You are asked by your employer to work non-compulsory overtime. You would naturally expect, and would be entitled to be paid, extra money for the additional hours you have worked, as you will have conferred a benefit on your employer and suffered a detriment in the bargain.

The general rule, however, was modified by the decision in Williams v Roffey Bros & Nicholls *[1991] 1 QB 1. The case concerned a contract to refurbish a block of flats. The defendants were the main contractors, and they subcontracted the carpentry work to the claimants for £20,000. Part way through the work the claimants realised they had underestimated the cost and told the defendants of their financial difficulty. The defendants (mindful of the fact that if the work was not completed on time they themselves would be liable to pay compensation under the main contract) promised to pay the claimants extra money (ie £575 per flat) to complete on time. On this basis the claimants continued to work on the flats but in the event were not paid the extra money promised by the defendants and sued. The main issue before the Court of Appeal was what, if any, consideration the claimants had given in return for the promise of additional money. Whilst it was conceded by the defendants that they had secured practical benefits (ie avoiding liability under the compensation clause in the main contract and the cost and expense of finding other carpenters to finish the job), the defendants argued that there was no legal benefit. The court held on the facts that the practical benefit per se was consideration.*

Figure 3.2 Alteration promises to pay more

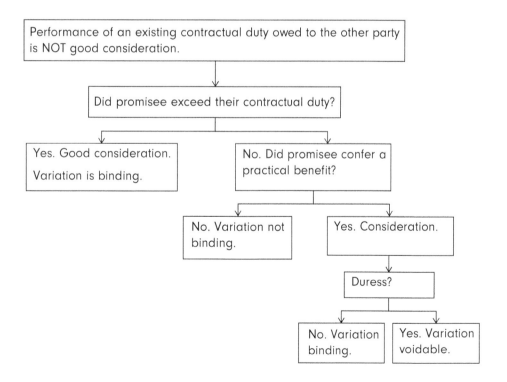

In practice, finding a practical benefit may not be difficult. Why would a business offer to pay extra money for something if it did *not* see a practical benefit in so doing? The only reason might be if the promise had been made under duress, in which case the variation may be avoided (covered in **Chapter 12**). However, all we are interested in at the moment is being able to identify when, and to what extent, performance of an existing contractual duty owed to the other party may be regarded as sufficient consideration for a promise of extra payment (see **Figure 3.2**).

3.3.1 Alteration promises to pay more – summary

- As a general rule, performance of an existing contractual duty owed to the other party is not consideration for a promise of extra payment.
- Exceeding a contractual duty is consideration.
- Performance of an existing contractual duty owed to the other party will be consideration for a promise of extra payment if it confers a practical benefit; however, if the promise to pay more was made under duress the promise may be set aside (see **Chapter 12**).

3.4 Alteration promises to accept less

3.4.1 Rule in *Pinnel's Case*

In the case of an undisputed debt, at common law, an agreement between a creditor and a debtor that the creditor will simply accept part payment in full and final settlement of the full amount is not binding on the creditor. This is the so-called 'rule in *Pinnel's Case*'.

 We will return to Pinnel's Case *itself in a moment, but first we are going to look at the leading case in this area, namely* Foakes v Beer *(1884) 9 App Cas 605.*

Dr Foakes owed Mrs Beer a fixed sum of money on which she was legally entitled to be paid interest. They then entered into an agreement concerning how Dr Foakes was going to pay Mrs Beer what he owed. In consideration of Dr Foakes paying off the capital by instalments, Mrs Beer agreed to forgo the interest. She later changed her mind though and sued for it. The question for the court was, had Dr Foakes given any consideration for her promise to forgo the interest? The answer was 'no' because no new consideration had been given by Dr Foakes for her promise to let him off the interest. Payment of the capital in instalments was only satisfying part of his debt, so Mrs Beer was entitled to change her mind and sue him for the interest.

3.4.1.1 Common law exception to the rule in *Pinnel's Case*

Remember the rule – consideration must be sufficient, but need not be adequate. Provided a debtor gives the creditor something (other than just part payment) in return for the creditor's promise to forgo the balance of the debt then that something different will be consideration. In *Pinnel's Case*, for example, the creditor agreed to accept part payment because it was paid in advance of the due date (which was a benefit to the creditor). The court in *Pinnel's Case* also spoke in terms of a 'horse, hawk or robe' being consideration for a creditor's promise to accept part payment. Whatever a 'horse, hawk or robe' might be worth, they each have some value, and if a creditor is happy to accept one, or other, in return for part (or no payment) so be it.

So at common law, unless there is some consideration for the concession, a debtor is at risk of the creditor changing their mind. This is where the equitable doctrine of promissory estoppel comes in.

3.4.2 Promissory estoppel

Under this doctrine, a creditor may be prevented ('estopped') from going back on a promise to accept part payment (even if the promise is not supported by consideration) if in all the circumstances it would be unfair for the creditor to do so.

Promissory estoppel is simply the idea that

- if you have made a promise not to enforce your legal rights; and
- someone has relied on that promise, even though they have not provided anything in return; then
- if you try to enforce your legal rights you will be 'estopped' (prevented from going back on your promise) if it would be inequitable (unfair) in all the circumstances to do so.

The doctrine of promissory estoppel is founded on the judgment of Denning J in the well-known case of Central London Property Trust v High Trees House *[1947] KB 130 (generally referred to as* 'High Trees'*). The basic facts of the case were:*

Lease entered into in 1937 – annual ground rent of £2,500 (payable quarterly).

January 1940 – agreement by landlord to accept £1,250 per annum (due to very low level of letting, arising from wartime conditions).

The defendants paid the reduced rent throughout the war.

By June 1945 all the flats were fully let.

In 1946 the landlord sought to recover back rent for the last two quarters of 1945 and full rent for the future.

So there were basically three 'periods' the court considered:

- *Period 1: unclaimed rent from the beginning of the war until the flats were fully let.*
- *Period 2: unclaimed rent for last two quarters of 1945 after the war had ended.*
- *Period 3: claiming reinstatement of full rent for the future.*

The court said obiter that the unclaimed rent for period 1 (the war period) was not recoverable, but held that as the concession had come to an end by early 1945 the unclaimed rent for the other two periods when the war had ended was recoverable.

So promissory estoppel may apply to prevent the enforcement of strict legal rights in circumstances where it would be unfair (inequitable) to do so. Note, however, the following limitations to the doctrine:

(a) It can only be used as a *defence* when a party brings an action at common law to enforce their legal rights.

(b) There must have been a promise to waive strict legal rights.

(c) The promisee (usually a debtor) must have acted on the promise but not necessarily to their detriment. For example the debtor in *High Trees* simply paid half rent.

(d) With ongoing payments such as rent, the doctrine operates to suspend the strict legal right, which means the creditor can resume their right to full payment going forward by giving *reasonable notice*. What the creditor cannot do is claim any back payments for the concessionary period. Hence why in *High Trees* the landlord could claim full rent for the future (it was deemed reasonable notice had been given) but could not claim arrears during the war period.

(e) To use any equitable doctrine a party must have 'clean hands'. So in a case where the debtor sought to take advantage of the creditor's financial difficulties, the debtor was

Contract

unable to use promissory estoppel as a defence to the creditor's common law action for the balance owed.

In relation to (d) above it is not known exactly what the position is in relation to part payment of a one-off debt. The consensus of academic opinion is that the doctrine operates to merely suspend the creditor's right to the balance owed, which can be resumed provided *reasonable notice* is given. What amounts to reasonable notice will depend very much on the facts.

3.4.3 Alteration promises to accept less – summary

- Part payment of a debt is not consideration for a promise to accept less.
- A common law exception? If so, the agreed variation is binding.
- If not, can promissory estoppel be raised as a defence?

Figure 3.3 shows how these points work together.

Figure 3.3 Alteration promises to pay less

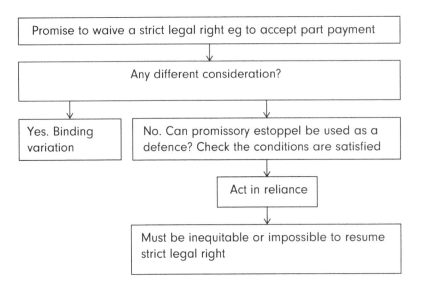

Summary

- For a contract and contractual variation to be binding there must be agreement, intention to create legal relations and consideration.
- Consideration is something given in return for a promise. It is often a promise to do something (executory consideration) although with unilateral contracts the consideration will be the specified act (executed consideration).
- Consideration must be sufficient in the eyes of the law. It need not adequately reflect the value of the promise for which it is given.
- Consideration must not be past, although if certain conditions are satisfied a past act/promise may be consideration.
- Performance of an existing public duty is not consideration. Exceeding a public duty is consideration.
- Performance of an existing duty owed to the other party is not consideration unless it confers a real practical benefit. If it confers a practical benefit the promise to pay more will be binding unless it was obtained by duress (see **Chapter 12**).

- Exceeding a contractual duty owed to the other party is consideration.
- Part payment of a debt is not consideration for a promise to accept less. If a new element is given in addition to part payment (eg payment early) that will be consideration. In any event query whether promissory estoppel can be raised as a defence. Check the relevant conditions are satisfied.

Sample questions

Question 1

A client decided to set up his own wine bar. He employed a builder to fit out the kitchen for £10,000.

The builder did most of the work, but then told the client he had seriously underestimated the cost of materials and could not afford to complete the job. The client told him not to worry and offered an extra £700 if it would help. The builder said it would, and went on to complete the work. As a result the client was able to open the wine bar on schedule.

Which of the following statements best describes the client's legal position in relation to the builder?

A   The client is obliged to pay the builder £10,700 as the promise to pay more conferred a practical benefit.

B   The client is not obliged to pay the builder the extra £700 as the builder gave no consideration for it.

C   The client is not obliged to honour the alteration promise to pay more as it was the builder's responsibility to properly cost the work in the first place.

D   The client is obliged to pay the builder £10,700 as all contractual variations are binding in the absence of extortion.

E   The client is obliged to pay the builder only £10,000 because as a matter of public policy the builder should not be allowed to demand extra money for what he contracted to do.

Answer

The correct statement is A.

The problem lies with the attempted variation. For a variation the general rule is that there must be the same elements present as for making a contract. So D is wrong. C is wrong too because if all essential elements are present the variation will be binding.

Question here is what consideration has the builder provided?

Here the builder has just performed his existing contractual duty, which generally is not regarded as sufficient. If he had done something extra that would have been consideration. Performance of an existing duty may be sufficient if it confers a practical/commercial benefit and there was no duress.

The client offered the money and arguably got a practical benefit by getting work finished so that the wine bar could open on time (*Williams v Roffey Bros.*). There was no evidence of duress (which you will look at in **Chapter 12**). Hence B is wrong.

No duress and so the client would most likely have to pay the extra £700.

E is wrong as it is not a public policy issue.

Contract

Question 2

A client has been running a business for a while but it has been making a steady loss. Two months ago with a view to making financial savings the client approached his landlord and asked if he would reduce the rent 'until things picked up'.

As a gesture of goodwill, the landlord agreed to reduce the rent by 25% (ie to £1,500 per month). So when the last two rent payments fell due the client only paid £1,500. Then yesterday the landlord told the client he had changed his mind and would be expecting the client to pay full rent in the future plus the arrears.

Which of the following statements best describes the legal position of the client with his landlord?

A   The client will have to pay £1,000 in arrears of rent and full rent in the future as he gave no consideration for the landlord's promise to reduce the rent.

B   The landlord suspended his right to full rent but can now demand full rent going forward even if things have not 'picked up'.

C   The client may raise promissory estoppel as a defence to any action brought by the landlord and the landlord will have to give reasonable notice to resume his legal right to receive full rent in the future.

D   At common law the client is not obliged to pay the arrears but must pay full rent in future.

E   As the landlord's promise was simply 'a gesture of goodwill' it would not be binding and he can now demand all outstanding monies.

Answer

The correct statement is C.

The question is whether or not the variation is binding. To be binding there must be agreement, consideration and contractual intention. Here the only issue is with consideration.

Part payment of a debt is not good consideration for a promise to forgo the balance (*Pinnel's Case*). On that basis the client has not given consideration for the landlord's promise to reduce the rent by 25% and so is bound to pay the arrears and full rent going forward. This explains why D is wrong.

There are common law exceptions, such as different consideration, but there is nothing on the facts to suggest that any of them apply. The landlord agreed to reduce the rent as a gesture of goodwill, which reinforces the conclusion that no consideration was given for the promise to accept less.

Consequently the client will have to try and rely on the equitable doctrine of promissory estoppel as a defence if he is sued for the full rent.

There must have been a promise by the landlord to waive a strict legal right intending the client to act on it. Here the landlord promised to waive his right to full rent and the client altered his position by paying the reduced rent.

Looking at *High Trees* the doctrine operates to suspend legal rights as to the future provided reasonable notice is given. In relation to the reduced rental payments made over the last two months it would seem that the landlord's right to the extra 25% will have been extinguished.

To use promissory estoppel the client would need to have 'clean hands'. On the facts there is nothing to suggest otherwise.

As the client may well be able to use promissory estoppel as a defence statements A, B and E are all wrong.

Question 3

A client decided to set up his own cafe. He took a lease of premises and asked his sister, owner of '1st Choice Blinds', to supply and fit a large awning at the back of the premises to provide extra covered seating for customers. His sister agreed and made and fitted the awning. The client was delighted with what she had done and said he would give her £1,000 for her trouble.

Which of the following statements best describes the legal position of the client in relation to his sister?

A   The client is not obliged to pay his sister £1,000 as she gave no consideration for the promise.

B   The client is not obliged to pay his sister £1,000 as there was no intention to create legal relations.

C   Your client is legally obliged to pay his sister £1,000 because it was a business-to-business arrangement.

D   The client's sister may have given sufficient consideration for the promise of £1,000 but it is unclear on the facts.

E   The client's sister is entitled to £1,000 as she was asked to do the work and it was mutually understood she would get paid for it.

Answer

D is correct.

On the face of it what the sister did looks like past consideration (which is not good consideration) but the exception may apply (*Re Casey's Patents*). The act was done at the client's request. Query whether it was mutually understood that she would get something for what she did. It looks like a large job. Had the promise been made in advance would it have been legally enforceable? This will hinge on contractual intention. With family arrangements (eg between brother and sister) there is a rebuttable presumption the parties did not intend to create legal relations; whereas in a commercial context (business-to-business), which it looks like here, there is a very strong presumption the parties intended legal relations (**see Chapter 2**).

This explains why D is correct and why the other statements, which categorically say the sister is or is not entitled to £1,000, are inaccurate.

4 Parties

4.1	Introduction	34
4.2	Privity of contract	34
4.3	Contracts (Rights of Third Parties) Act 1999	34
4.4	Agency	35

SQE1 syllabus

This chapter will enable you to achieve the SQE1 assessment specification in relation to functioning legal knowledge concerned with identifying the parties to a contract and anyone else who may have rights and liabilities under it.

Note that, for SQE1, candidates are not usually required to recall specific case names or cite statutory or regulatory authorities. Cases are provided for illustrative purposes only.

Learning outcomes

By the end of this chapter you will be able to apply relevant core legal principles and rules appropriately and effectively, at the level of a competent newly qualified solicitor in practice, to realistic client-based and ethical problems and situations in the following areas:

- recognising whether a third party has acquired the benefit of a contract under the Contracts (Rights of Third Parties) Act (C(RTP)A) 1999; and
- recognising whether an agent has authority to bind someone else to a contract.

4.1 Introduction

In practice, it is really important to determine who are the parties to a transaction as the general rule is that only the contracting parties can have rights and liabilities under it.

Also in practice, agents often enter into contracts on behalf of someone else. For example if you book a holiday through a travel agent, the holiday contract is between you and the tour operator – the agent is not a party to the resulting contract and just drops out of the picture. Agency is particularly important in commercial law. Companies (as separate legal entities) inevitably need flesh-and-blood individuals (directors) to act for them in order to enter contracts. Agency law determines how that power (authority) is given to parties to bind companies and partnerships.

4.2 Privity of contract

In the last chapter we looked at consideration and the idea that to sue for breach of a particular promise you must have given consideration to the defaulting party for that promise. This necessarily means that only a contracting party (ie someone who is privy to the contract) can sue for breach of contract or otherwise be liable for breach. This general rule is referred to as privity of contract, ie only the actual parties to a contract are bound by it and therefore have rights and obligations under it.

This rule of privity effectively meant that third parties could neither sue nor be sued on a contract. As far as contractual obligations go, no one has ever really questioned the rule, but what about benefits under a contract? What if a contract has been made for the benefit of a third party? The privity rule meant that the third party still had no rights under the contract.

 This is illustrated by the old case of Tweddle v Atkinson *(1861) 1 B & S 393. The claimant was engaged to be married and his father and future father-in-law made a contract providing that each of them would give a certain sum of money to the claimant. Even though the contract expressly provided that the claimant was to be entitled to enforce it, the court held that he could not do so.*

It is this aspect of the rule that has been criticised and, needless to say, ways around it have emerged over the years. The main exception was introduced by the C(RTP)A 1999, which we look at next.

4.3 Contracts (Rights of Third Parties) Act 1999

Under this Act, a third party can acquire rights if:

- the contract expressly provides that they may acquire a benefit (s 1(1)(a)); or
- the term purports to confer a benefit on them (s 1(1)(b)).

Subsection (1)(b) does not apply, however, if on a true construction of the contract it was not intended that the term be enforceable by a third party (s 1(2)). For a third party to enforce a term of the contract in their own right, they must be expressly identified in the contract by name or as a member of a class (eg 'employees') or answering a particular description.

This Act explains why, in the run up to Christmas, shops will often ask if you would like a gift receipt for goods you are buying. If you say you are buying the goods for a friend or family member you thereby confer direct contractual rights on the recipient so if something happens to be wrong with the goods the recipient (rather than you) can take them back to the shop and seek a remedy. We will be looking at remedies under contracts for the sale of goods in **Chapter 6**.

The Act also extends to the benefit of exemption clauses, which we will also be looking at in **Chapter 6**.

4.4 Agency

Appointment of commercial agents to negotiate and/or to enter into deals on another's behalf is common in practice; but an agent can only bind someone to a deal if the agent has authority to do so. All agents are given express authority to do particular things, but sometimes they may act outside that authority. The question then arises as to whether the agent had any other type of authority, eg implied authority through a custom of the trade.

Agency is a very common feature of business and commercial life. If you are in business, you cannot always do everything for yourself. Sometimes you need the expertise of others to conduct dealings on your behalf and companies need individuals (directors) to act for them. The directors may delegate powers to management.

Agents all have one thing in common: they are persons who have the ability or power to change the legal relations of the person for whom they are the agent. This person is called the principal. The person with whom the agent contracts, on behalf of the principal, is called the third party.

Normally when contract lawyers use the term 'third party', they just mean somebody who is not party to the contract they are concerned with. But in the context of agency, the term is used differently. When we talk about a 'third party' in the law of agency, we are referring to someone who is a third party to the *relationship* of agency between the principal and the agent. But the third party is *not* 'a third party' in the normal sense, standing outside the contract formed with the principal; the whole point is that they *are* party to the contract with the principal.

Examples of agents include:

- Travel agents
- Insurance brokers
- Ticket agents
- Shop assistants
- Auctioneers
- Company directors

On the other hand, note that lots of persons who get called 'agents' may not be agents in the strict legal sense. For example, estate agents do not normally contract to sell property on behalf of their clients – they only tend to have authority to advertise the property for sale and facilitate the reaching of an agreement. So be aware that the commercial use of the word 'agent' is not always the same as the legal use of it.

The simplest way in which agency can be created is by the principal giving the required authority to the agent to contract on its behalf.

4.4.1 Actual authority

The actual authority of an agent is worked out by looking at what the parties have said and done, and any relevant surrounding circumstances.

This authority can be granted expressly, or it can be implied. For example, an agent may have the express authority to sell certain products, but also implied actual authority to do things usually carried out by sellers of goods eg advertise them and receive payment for them. This is all agreed between the principal and the agent and most agents have a contract of some sort with their principal.

But sometimes, agents purport to act for their principals in circumstances where they do not have actual authority. This may happen for a variety of reasons – because agents do not always do exactly as they are told; because they are unsure of the extent of their authority; or even because, although they *did* have authority, it has been *revoked* in some way, eg because the principal has become ill or died.

Nonetheless, there are some circumstances where the law regards the acts of the agent as binding on the principal, despite the lack of actual authority. The third party, believing they have entered into a contract with the principal, may claim there is a binding agreement, and the principal may argue to the contrary, because the purported agent had no right to contract on their behalf.

4.4.2 Apparent authority

Here the agent does not have actual authority from the principal. But the agent could still be able to form a binding contract, because they have a different form of authority – one which has been made apparent to the third party by the principal. It is not sufficient that the so-called 'agent' appears to be authorised. The appearance of authority must be created by the principal and this representation must have been intended to be and in fact was acted upon by the other party.

So for apparent (or what is sometimes called ostensible) authority to arise the following three conditions must be satisfied:

- at some stage the principal must have represented (by words or conduct) that the agent had authority;
- the third party must rely on this representation, believing that the agent has authority; and
- the third party must alter their position eg by entering into a contract.

⊙ Example

When Paul started up a business manufacturing wooden toys (including traditional rocking horses) he employed Abba Ltd as his selling agent for the toys. Paul agreed not to supply customers direct.

He instructed Abba Ltd to sell the rocking horses for at least £500 each. Nigel approached Paul direct to buy a rocking horse. Paul referred Nigel to Abba Ltd telling him that he had to deal through Paul's agent, Abba Ltd. Abba Ltd contracted to sell a rocking horse to Nigel for £400. Paul refuses to sell for that amount.

But is Paul legally obliged to sell it to Nigel for £400? This hinges on whether Abba Ltd was authorised to enter into the contract with Nigel on Paul's behalf and so bind Paul. Provided Abba Ltd had authority, Abba Ltd would acquire no rights or liabilities under the contract. The contract would be between Paul and Nigel.

Authority may be actual or apparent. Abba Ltd had express authority to sell the rocking horses but for at least £500 each. Abba Ltd exceeded its authority and so had no express authority to do the deal.

As Paul told Nigel to deal through Abba Ltd and did not mention any express limitation on Abba's authority, Nigel would think Abba Ltd had authority to sell him a rocking horse for £400, ie Abba Ltd had apparent authority. Paul would be estopped from denying, as against Nigel, that Abba Ltd had authority to sell the rocking horse for £400.

Consequently, Paul is bound to sell the horse to Nigel for £400; otherwise he will be in breach of contract. Abba Ltd has no rights or liabilities under the contract of sale, but will be liable to Paul for breach of the agency agreement.

Whilst the statutory rights under the C(RTP)A 1999 represent an exception to the doctrine of privity, the same is not true of agency. An authorised agent has no rights (or indeed obligations) under the resulting contract. The agent is authorised to enter the contract on behalf of someone else (called the principal) and the resulting contract is between the principal and other party. The agent simply drops out of the picture.

Summary

- As a general rule only parties to the contract have rights and liabilities under it. This is the rule of privity.
- A third party may acquire the benefit of a contract if it was clearly intended that they should be able to enforce it and was identified by name or as a member of a particular class (C(RTP)A 1999).
- An authorised agent may bind the principal to a contract (**Figure 4.1**). An agent may have actual (express or implied) authority or authority may arise by estoppel. This is where the principal gave the distinct but false impression the agent had authority and the third party relied on that representation.

Figure 4.1 Parties and contracts in an agency arrangement

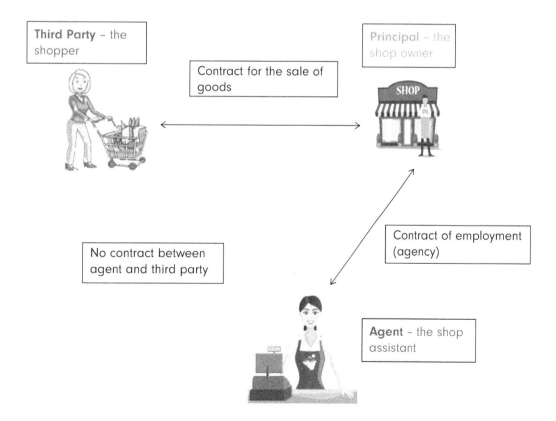

Contract

Sample questions

Question 1

A client owns a car dealership and sells high value, nearly new cars to business customers looking to purchase company cars. The Sales Manager can agree to sell a maximum of three cars in any transaction. Any larger transaction must first be approved by the Finance Officer. Last week, the Sales Manager agreed to sell five sports cars to a valued customer with delivery agreed to be made next week. The client has now been informed of the transaction by the Finance Officer, who found out about it yesterday and had not approved it.

Which of the following statements best describes whether the client will be in breach of contract if they do not perform the contract?

A   No, because the Sales Manager did not have authority to enter the contract.

B   No, because the contract has not yet been completed and can be revoked.

C   Yes, because the Sales Manager had actual authority to enter the contract.

D   Yes, because the client represented to the customer that the Sales Manager had authority to enter the contract.

E   Yes, because the Sales Manager represented to the customer that he had authority to enter the contract.

Answer

The correct option is D. The Sales Manager (SM) is likely to have apparent authority to act as the client's agent. There is a representation that the client (as principal) has made to the customer that the SM had authority to agree the sale of the five cars. It is likely this is created by the SM being in charge at the showroom and the customer having made previous purchases there. The customer has relied on this representation believing the SM had authority to enter the contract and the customer has altered his position by entering into the contract to buy the cars.

It must be the principal who makes the representation, not the agent, so E is wrong.

A is wrong as apparent authority is likely to exist here and C is wrong as the actual authority to sell this number of cars has not been given to the SM on the facts.

B is wrong as the contract is already formed so the client will be in breach if the client does not perform it.

Question 2

A client owns a pub and employs someone to manage it. The manager is the exclusive face of the business; his name is on the bar and the licence of the pub. The client explicitly instructed the manager not to make any purchases outside of bottled ales and mineral waters, but the manager entered into an agreement for the purchase of cigars and in the event did not pay for them. The seller of the cigars discovered the client is the actual owner of the business and is suing the client for the price.

Which of the following statements best describes whether the client will be liable to the seller?

A   Yes, because the manager had apparent/ostensible authority to buy the cigars.

B   Yes, because the manager had implied actual authority as buying cigars is within the range of acts usually carried out by a pub manager.

C   Yes, because the manager represented he had authority and the seller relied on that representation and entered into the contract.

D   No, because the manager had neither actual (express or implied) nor apparent authority to buy the cigars.

E   No, because the agent had deliberately acted outside his express authority.

Answer

The correct statement is B. Buying cigars is within the usual authority of pub managers and so the manager had implied actual authority to buy them. The facts of the scenario are based on *Watteau v Fenwick* [1893] 1 QB 346.

A is wrong because there was no holding out by the client as principal. The seller was unaware of the principal at the time of the sale.

C is wrong because there was no representation of authority by the agent and for apparent authority the representation must come from the principal.

D is wrong because the agent had implied actual authority.

E is wrong because it is irrelevant whether or not the agent deliberately acted outside his authority.

5 Capacity

5.1	Introduction	42
5.2	Minors	42
5.3	Mental incapacity	43
5.4	Corporations	43

SQE1 syllabus

This chapter will enable you to achieve the SQE1 assessment specification in relation to functioning legal knowledge of the limited capacity (power) of some persons and organisations to enter a contract.

Note that, for SQE1, candidates are not usually required to recall specific case names or cite statutory or regulatory authorities. Cases are provided for illustrative purposes only.

Learning outcomes

By the end of this chapter you will be able to apply relevant core legal principles and rules appropriately and effectively, at the level of a competent newly qualified solicitor in practice, to realistic client-based and ethical problems and situations relating to:

- advising on contracts entered into by:
    - minors;
    - persons lacking mental capacity; and
    - corporations.

5.1 Introduction

In the last chapter we considered the doctrine of privity and the importance of identifying the parties to a contract. The general rule is that only parties to a contract can sue or be sued on it. Occasionally, though, a contract will not bind a party because the party lacked the necessary capacity or power to make a contract.

The main categories of people whose power, or capacity, to enter contracts is limited by law are minors (persons under the age of 18) and people with a mental incapacity eg due to a nervous breakdown or drunkenness.

Also it goes without saying that a contracting party should be a person recognised as such by the law. Persons in law, however, are not confined to individual adults. A lot of contracts are entered into by, or on behalf of, organisations such as companies and local authorities. Such bodies are generally called corporations and the capacity of a corporation depends on the type of corporation.

5.2 Minors

The basic common law principle is that minors are not bound by contracts they have entered – the other party is bound and can be sued, but not the minor. As with all general principles, though, there are exceptions. Contracts for 'necessaries' bind minors. 'Necessaries' include not just the supply of necessary goods and services, but also contracts of service for a minor's benefit (**Figure 5.1**).

'Necessaries' are defined under the SGA 1979 as goods 'suitable to the condition in life of the minor and to his actual requirements at the time of sale and delivery'. 'Necessaries' therefore extend beyond the absolute essentials (such as food and clothing). What is 'necessary' for a particular minor will depend to an extent on their social status *and* their actual requirements at the time of purchase.

⭐ Example

A bespoke tailor shop supplies an expensive blazer to a 16-year-old boy, Michael, who comes from a wealthy family. The contract might be binding on Michael. It will depend on whether, or not, he already has an adequate supply of blazers and the like.

Minors are also bound by contracts of service that are, on the whole, beneficial to them. Generally this refers to contracts of employment under which a minor gains training and experience (eg an apprenticeship) as long as, on balance, the contract is more favourable than not to the minor.

Figure 5.1 Capacity of minors

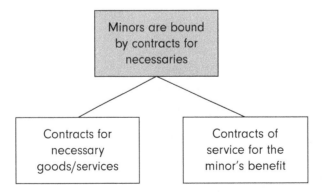

This point is illustrated by Proform Sports Management Ltd v Proactive Sports Management *[2006] EWHC 2903 (Ch) a.k.a. the 'Wayne Rooney case'. When Wayne Rooney, aged 15 years, was playing for Everton FC, he entered into a two-year contract with Proform to act as his agent. Before the end of the two years he terminated the contract. The court held he was entitled to do so as the contract with Proform (unlike the contract with Everton FC) was not a contract for necessaries.*

5.3 Mental incapacity

This category covers persons suffering from mental impairment and those who are drunk when the contract is made. Generally, contracts made with someone in either state will be valid unless at the time the contract was made the person was incapable of understanding the nature of the transaction *and* the other party knew that to be the case. In such instances the contract will be 'voidable', which means it is binding unless, and until, the person suffering from the mental impairment or inebriation terminates it. We will be considering voidable contracts in **Chapters 11** and **12**.

 Example

An elderly gentleman, Jack, entered into a contract with Hansaj. Unknown to Hansaj, Jack was suffering from senile dementia. Even if Jack did not understand the nature of the deal he had struck, he would be bound by it as Hansaj was unaware of Jack's mental incapacity.

The final type of legal 'person' that may lack capacity is a corporation, which we are going to look at next.

5.4 Corporations

If two or more people form themselves into an association for the purpose of some concerted enterprise (eg a club or a trading company), the association is in some cases regarded by the law as being an independent person called a corporation. A corporation is treated by the law as having a separate legal identity from the person, or persons, who constitute it. Note, however, that not all associations are corporations: it depends on whether, or not, they have been incorporated by the state. An unincorporated association, such as a club, is not a competent contracting party. If a contract is made on its behalf no individual member can be sued on it except the person who actually made it and any other member who authorised them to do so.

The three main types of corporation are:

- Registered companies
- Statutory corporations
- Limited liability partnerships

5.4.1 Registered companies

Most companies are registered under the Companies Act (CA) 2006. Section 31 of the CA 2006 allows a company to carry on whatever activity it wants (within the law, of course). Further, s 39 of the CA 2006 effectively abolishes the 'ultra vires' doctrine with regard to third parties dealing with the company. In other words, s 39 provides that an act undertaken by the company with an outsider (such as entering a contract) cannot be challenged if it is beyond the powers granted in the company's constitution. Both the company and the other party to the transaction are bound by the Act. This is backed up by s 40(1), which states that the powers of the directors to bind a company (eg by entering a contract) are deemed to be free of any limitation under the company's constitution in favour of a person dealing with the company in good faith. Notwithstanding that, parties looking to enter into a contract with a company are still best advised to check the company's capacity.

5.4.2 Statutory corporations

These corporations (as their name suggests) are created by statute. They include local authorities. The statute creating each corporation will set out the purposes for which the corporation may enter contracts. Any contract entered outside of the stated powers will be declared ultra vires and therefore void.

5.4.3 Limited liability partnerships

This form of corporation was created by the Limited Liability Partnerships Act 2000 and such partnerships benefit from unlimited capacity.

Summary

- As a general rule, minors are not bound by contracts unless it is a contract for 'necessaries'. Even if a minor is not bound by a contract through lack of capacity, the other party will be bound by it.
- Persons suffering from a mental impairment or intoxication will not be bound by a contract if they did not comprehend the nature of the deal *and* the other party was aware of that.
- Corporations have different levels of contracting ability, eg a statutory corporation will not be bound by contracts that are outside its statutory powers whilst limited liability partnerships have unlimited capacity.

Sample question

Question 1

A girl, aged 17 years, is keen on performing arts and decides to pursue a career in it. She sets up a small business selling dance and stage clothing. The money she makes from the business pays for singing and dancing lessons. After a few months the girl's main supplier discovers she is only 17 years of age and refuses to deal with her. This leaves the girl without enough business to pay for this month's lessons. Her tutor is pressing her for payment. The girl is also in arrears with her mobile phone account.

Which of the following statements best describes the girl's legal position in relation to one or other of the contracts she has entered?

A   The contract for the supply of the stage clothes was not binding on the girl as it was a trading contract.

B   The contract for the singing and dancing lessons would not be binding on the girl as it was not a contract for necessaries.

C   The girl can terminate the mobile phone contract and the contract for the singing and dancing lessons.

D   The girl is bound by the contracts for the clothes she sells as she needs the proceeds of sales to pay for her lessons.

E   The mobile phone contract would be deemed a contract for necessaries and as such it would bind the girl but not the mobile phone company.

Answer

The correct option is A. The contract for the supply of the clothes to her and the contracts of resale would not bind the girl as they are trading contracts. These contracts are not contracts for necessaries. This explains why D is wrong.

B is wrong because the contract for the lessons looks like a contract for necessaries, as it is a contract of service that is on the whole for her benefit.

C is wrong as both contracts are likely to be deemed to be contracts for necessaries.

E is wrong because although the phone contract may well be deemed a contract for necessaries the mobile phone company would be bound by the contract in any event.

PART 2
CONTENTS

6 Contents

6.1	Express terms	50
6.2	Implied terms	54

SQE1 syllabus

This chapter will enable you to achieve the SQE1 assessment specification in relation to functioning legal knowledge concerned with the content of contracts. This includes express and implied terms and the classification of terms.

Note that, for SQE1, candidates are not usually required to recall specific case names or cite statutory or regulatory authorities. Cases are provided for illustrative purposes only.

Learning outcomes

By the end of this chapter you will be able to apply relevant core legal principles and rules appropriately and effectively, at the level of a competent newly qualified solicitor in practice, to realistic client-based and ethical problems and situations in the following areas:

- identifying the express and implied terms of a contract; and
- classifying contract terms to advise on the remedies available for breach.

6.1 Express terms

Working out what are the terms that the parties have expressly agreed seems a simple idea and it often is. For example, you go into a shop and buy a particular item for the stated price. The express terms are the item and the price. Working out the express terms is also easy where the parties agree and sign a written contract.

But we are going to concentrate on the main area of difficulty, namely what is often referred to as 'small print' (eg terms and conditions on notices and printed on the back of documents) and how they get to be part of the contract. When you order a holiday from a brochure, how and why do the terms and conditions become part of the contract? What about when you buy a cinema ticket, and you do not sign anything at all? Does the contract include the 'terms and conditions' on the back of the ticket?

6.1.1 Incorporation of terms

Terms may be incorporated into a contract in the following ways:

- Signature
- Reasonable notice before or at the time of the contract
- A previous consistent course of dealing

6.1.1.1 Signature

Basically, if you sign a contract, you are bound by it. For example, if you have ever borrowed money, you probably signed a loan agreement that included the words 'I have read and understood the terms and conditions overleaf'. The chances are you have not read and understood them but, generally speaking, you will be bound by the terms and conditions because you have shown your assent to them by signing. The same could be said for a box on screen that you have ticked to confirm you have read and understood all the terms and conditions of a contract made online. It is only in unusual circumstances – eg the term is illegible, or particularly onerous and not reasonably drawn to the other party's attention, or otherwise the contents of the document have been misrepresented – that this rule would not apply. We will look at misrepresentation in **Chapter 11**.

6.1.1.2 Reasonable notice

It is not as easy to assess whether the terms of a document that has not been signed should be regarded as incorporated into the contract. This is often the case, for example, if terms are contained in notices at the point of sale or transaction, or are on the back of tickets. In these cases, the law generally requires the party who wants to rely on the term to have given *reasonable notice at or before the time of the contract*. If reasonable notice of a term *has* been given, then the law will regard it as incorporated into the contract. If not, then it will not be.

Factors the courts take into account in deciding whether, or not, reasonable notice has been given are:

- Nature of the document. Is the document one on which a reasonable person would expect there to be contract terms? For example, a term on the back of a ticket that someone had been given after paying for the hire of a deckchair was held not to be a term of the contract. A reasonable person would simply have assumed that the ticket was proof of payment.

- Timing. The notice must come before or at the time of the contract (eg on a quotation) and not afterwards (eg on an invoice).

- Onerous terms (eg a term imposing a substantial fine if a particular condition is not met). The more onerous the term the more a party must do to bring it to the other party's attention. As a famous judge once said, 'Some clauses which I have seen would need to be printed in red ink on the face of the document with a red hand pointing to them before the notice could be held to be sufficient'.

- The exemption clause must be legible.
- If the term is set out on the back of a document are there words on the front drawing the other party's attention to them, such as 'See terms overleaf'?

6.1.1.3 Previous consistent course of dealing

The last way in which terms may become incorporated in a contract is by virtue of a previous consistent course of dealing. For terms to be incorporated in this way the parties must have had a lot of regular dealings in the past that were all on exactly the same terms and conditions, the premise being that by this stage in their dealings the parties should be familiar with those terms and conditions (even if on each individual occasion they have been provided after the contract, for example in an invoice).

Examples

Situation	Incorporation?
The parties have had three or four dealings over the last five years always on the same terms.	There will not have been sufficient past dealings for the innocent party to be expected to remember the terms they had contracted on in the past.
The parties have had lots of dealings in the past but there has been no consistency; sometimes, but not always, one party has been asked to sign a document containing terms.	Notwithstanding the regularity of the dealings there has been no consistency. On any given occasion, the party alleging breach would have no idea in advance what would be the terms and conditions on which the other party sought to contract. Sometimes there might be a signed document containing terms, but no guarantee there will be one.
The parties have had dealings three or four times a year over a long period of time and a sale note has routinely been handed over, which sets out the seller's standard terms and conditions.	Terms are likely to be incorporated by virtue of the parties' regular and consistent dealings.

6.1.1.4 Incorporation of terms – summary

The legal principles for determining incorporation of terms (**Figure 6.1**) apply to all types of terms buried in small print. In practice, however, they have proven particularly problematic in relation to exemption clauses (see **Chapter 7**). It is these clauses that usually cause disputes between parties, which is why whether, or not, they are included in the contract becomes so important.

6.1.2 Classification of terms

Once you have decided what the terms of a contract are it may be important to classify the type of term that has been breached. If the claimant simply wants damages then there is no need to do so as damages are available for every breach of contract. But what if the claimant wants to terminate (end) the contract as well as claim damages? Termination is only available in limited circumstances, eg if an important term of the contract (called a 'condition') has been breached and there are outstanding contractual obligations.

Traditionally terms were either classified as 'conditions' (important terms) or 'warranties' (minor terms). If conditions are breached prima facie the innocent party can terminate the

Figure 6.1 Incorporation of terms

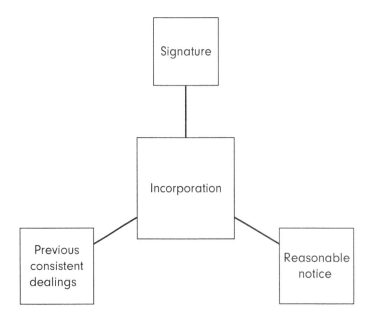

future performance of the contract as well as claim damages. Even if the breach happens to be fairly insignificant the point is that an important term has been breached and for this reason alone the non-defaulting party has a choice whether to terminate or affirm the contract. Warranties, on the other hand, are minor terms. If a warranty is breached the only remedy is damages, however serious the breach.

Terms in a written contract may be specifically identified as conditions or warranties or otherwise a contract may specify what will be the consequences of breach. For example in sale and purchase agreements of businesses there will often be a raft of 'Warranties' in relation to particular aspects of the business – see below.

Extracts from a sale and purchase agreement

5. Warranties

The Seller warrants that, save as fully and clearly disclosed ... each of the Warranties set out in Schedule 7 is true and accurate.

...

Schedule 7: The Warranties

...

3. Litigation

Neither the Seller, nor any person for whose acts or omissions the Seller may be vicariously liable, is engaged in, subject to or threatened by any litigation, administrative, mediation or arbitration proceedings in relation to the Business, and there are no circumstances likely to lead to any litigation, administrative, mediation or arbitration against the Seller or by the Seller against any third party.

But be aware that where a written contract has been drafted by a non-lawyer, they may be blissfully unaware of the significance of calling a particular term, say, a 'condition'. It will then be a case of looking at all the circumstances and deciding whether, or not, the parties could have intended breach of the particular term to lead to the possibility of termination. So, do not take at face value what a term may be called in a contract, unless the contract has been drafted by lawyers.

Terms may also have been judicially recognised as being a condition or warranty. For example, case law has determined that 'expected ready to load' clauses in charter parties (contracts to hire ships) are conditions.

The traditional approach meant that parties could work out in advance what would be the consequences of a particular breach. Commercial parties in particular like this sort of certainty, but with that certainty comes inflexibility. What if breach of a condition is so slight that most people would regard termination as being unreasonable and out-of-proportion to the effect of the breach?

Hence the courts came to recognise 'innominate' or 'intermediate' terms.

 The case that is often said to have created the concept of innominate terms is Hong Kong Fir Shipping Co Ltd v Kawasaki Kisen Kaisha Ltd *[1962] 2 QB (CA). The particular term in question was a 'seaworthiness' clause in a contract for the hire of a ship. Such a clause may be breached in a spectrum of different ways ranging from the serious to the insignificant. So rather than classify such clauses at the outset the Court of Appeal introduced a 'wait and see' approach. In other words the remedy would depend on the ultimate effect of the breach. Only if the breach was really serious and effectively deprived the innocent party of substantially the whole benefit they expected to receive under the contract would they have the choice to terminate or affirm the contract.*

The only downside to this approach is the potential uncertainty of determining whether, or not, a breach in an ongoing contract is serious enough to justify the innocent party terminating the future performance of it.

 Example

*Ruhi is employed as a teacher. Under the terms of her contract she is entitled to three months' notice. She is instantly dismissed for alleged gross misconduct – in other words her contract of employment is terminated without notice. Ruhi sues her employer for wrongful dismissal (ie dismissal in breach of contract). If Ruhi can establish on the balance of probability that her behaviour fell short of gross misconduct then her employer will be liable for breach of contract and will have to pay compensation (damages) to Ruhi to cover her net loss over three months (ie the length of her notice). You will consider damages in **Chapter 8**.*

Figure 6.2 provides a quick summary.

Figure 6.2 Classification of terms

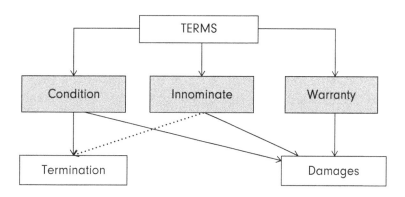

6.2 Implied terms

Invariably a contract is not simply the deal the parties have expressly agreed. The express terms are backed-up by terms implied by necessary implication to make sense of what has been expressly agreed. Terms that are so obvious they go without saying.

✪ *Examples*

1. When you buy something from a shop (eg an alarm clock) it is unlikely that you will specifically check with the shop that the item actually works. But what if your new goods prove faulty as soon as you get them home? You would no doubt take the goods back to the shop and demand a refund. On what basis? The shop did not expressly promise that your goods would work and you did not check. Why? Because it goes without saying that new goods bought from a shop should be fit for their purpose and free from defects.

2. You enter into a contract with a builder to build a house for you. What if they built the house on sand rather than concrete? Could the builder deny liability on the basis you never asked for concrete? Of course not. It goes without saying that the builder should exercise reasonable skill and judgement when constructing something for you. That's exactly why you did not specify concrete foundations, rather than sand foundations.

One reason for implying terms into a contract is to reflect what the parties have implicitly agreed anyway. Contract law is about giving effect to the intention of the parties – their *implied* intentions as well as their *express* ones.

So when do terms get implied into contracts? There are four main categories:

- Terms implied by custom
- Terms implied in fact
- Terms implied in law
- Terms implied by statute

6.2.1 Terms implied at common law

6.2.1.1 Terms implied by custom

A term may be implied if it reflects what are regarded as the well-known and legally binding customs of a particular trade. Note, however, that a term will not be implied by custom if it would contradict an express term of the contract.

6.2.1.2 Terms implied in fact

Here, a term may be implied into a contract where the parties have not expressly agreed something, but the contract would be unworkable without the relevant term. It is taken that the parties have implicitly agreed what is necessary to make commercial sense of their contract. Something that is so obvious it goes without saying.

6.2.1.3 Terms implied in law

Here, a term may be implied into a contract because the law regards it as a necessary incident of a particular type of contract. For example, in an employment contract, there is an implied duty on the employer to provide a healthy and safe environment for the employee to work in; and a duty on the employee to provide an honest and loyal service. The law sees these things as essential to an employment relationship.

6.2.2 Terms implied by statute

In some ways, this is really a 'sub-category' of terms implied in law. But we will treat it separately because it is by far the most important way in which terms get implied into contracts.

6.2.2.1 Terms implied by statute into business-to-business contracts for the sale and supply of goods and/or services

The relevant statutes are the SGA 1979 and the Supply of Goods and Services Act (SGSA) 1982. **Table 6.1** sets out some of the main sections of the SGA 1979.

Table 6.1 Sale of Goods Act 1979 implied terms

Sale of Goods Act 1979

12(1) In a contract of sale ... there is an implied term on the part of the seller that ... he has a right to sell the goods.

13(1) Where there is a contract for the sale of goods by description, there is an implied term that the goods will correspond with the description.

14(2) Where the seller sells goods in the course of a business, there is an implied term that the goods supplied under the contract are of satisfactory quality.

14(2A) ... goods are of satisfactory quality if they meet the standard that a reasonable person would regard as satisfactory, taking account of any description of the goods, the price (if relevant) and all the other relevant circumstances.

14(3) Where the seller sells goods in the course of a business and the buyer, expressly or by implication, makes known to the seller ... any particular purpose for which the goods are being bought, there is an implied term that the goods supplied under the contract are reasonably fit for that purpose, whether or not that is a purpose for which such goods are commonly supplied, except where the circumstances show that the buyer does not rely, or that it is unreasonable for him to rely, on the skill or judgment of the seller ...

⭐ *Example*

The owner of a public house, Gary, is on the internet looking to buy a large smart screen TV to mount on a wall in the bar so that customers can watch live sports coverage. He finds a suitable TV on the Supatelly company website. It is priced at £1,200. There is a description underneath the picture of the TV, stating its screen size and resolution, the inputs it can take and other details. Gary likes what he reads and orders one. He clicks on the 'I agree to Supatelly's terms and conditions' button, puts in his credit card details and in due course the new TV arrives.

So let's see what Gary agreed (expressly and impliedly) with Supatelly.

The express terms will be for the sale of the specified TV at the price of £1,200; together with the standard Supatelly terms and conditions to which Gary gave his agreement online.

What about the terms that will be implied into his contract by the SGA 1979?

Section 13(1) implied a term commonly referred to as 'correspondence with description'. The idea here is that if the TV has been sold 'by description' – as is likely to be the case here where the goods are described as having certain characteristics and specifications – then the buyer is entitled to something that corresponds with that description.

Section 14 implies two further terms into Gary's contract with Supatelly: section 14(2) implies a term that the goods will be of satisfactory quality *and section 14(3) implies a term that the goods will be* fit for purpose.

Note that ss 12, 13 and 14 of the SGA 1979 are all classified by the Act as 'conditions' and they impose strict liability (which means liability does not depend on fault by the seller). The fact that these terms are conditions means that if they are breached prima facie the innocent party can reject the goods and get a refund as well as claim damages. The only bars to rejecting the goods are:

(a) where the buyer has accepted the goods (eg they have intimated acceptance or otherwise kept the goods beyond a reasonable time without seeking to reject them); or

(b) in relation to ss 13 and 14, where the breach is so slight that it would be unreasonable to reject the goods.

Strict liability means that the seller need not personally be at fault for the goods not matching their description or otherwise being defective. The point is that for some reason the goods do not comply with one, or other, of the terms implied by the SGA 1979. The actual reason why is irrelevant.

As well as contracts for the sale of goods there are two other main types of contract, namely:

- contracts for a service/work (eg a furniture removal contract and logistics contract); and
- contracts that involve both the supply of work and materials (goods) (eg a contract to supply and fit a new kitchen).

The statute that implies terms into these contracts is the SGSA 1982. It implies certain terms in relation to the work/service supplied and terms almost identical to those in the SGA 1979 in relation to any goods supplied (see **Table 6.2**).

Table 6.2 Supply of Goods and Services Act 1982 implied terms

Supply of Goods and Services Act 1982	Type of business-to-business contract	Condition	Innominate term
2(1) In a contract for the transfer of goods, there is an implied condition on the part of the transferor that they have a right to transfer the property [ownership] in the goods.	Work and materials	√	
3 Where there is a supply of goods by description there is an implied term that the goods will correspond with that description.	Work and materials	√	
4(2) Where goods are supplied in the course of a business, it is an implied term that the goods will be of satisfactory quality.	Work and materials	√	
4(5) Where goods are supplied in the course of a business, and the buyer makes known to the supplier their purpose for the goods (either expressly or impliedly) and reasonably relies on the supplier's skill/knowledge, there is an implied term that the goods will be fit for that purpose.	Work and materials	√	
13 Where work or a service is done in the course of a business there is an implied term that it will be carried out with reasonable care and skill.	Work and materials and service contracts		√

Supply of Goods and Services Act 1982	Type of business-to-business contract	Condition	Innominate term
14 Where work or a service is done in the course of a business and no time for performance has been agreed, it is implied that the work will be done within a reasonable time.	Work and materials and service contracts		√
15 If a price for work or a service has not been fixed, there is an implied term that a reasonable sum will be charged.	Work and materials and service contracts		√

Note ss 13–15 do not impose strict liability and are innominate terms. Also the terms implied by ss 14 and 15 only apply in the absence of express agreement to the contrary.

6.2.2.2 Terms implied by statute into business-to-consumer contracts for the sale of goods and supply of goods and services

The relevant statute here is the Consumer Rights Act (CRA) 2015 (see **Table 6.3**).

Table 6.3 Consumer Rights Act 2015 implied terms

Consumer Rights Act 2015	Type of business-to-consumer contract
9 Where goods are sold/supplied in the course of a business, there is an implied term that the goods will be of satisfactory quality.	Sale of goods. Supply of goods under a goods and services contract.
10 Where goods are sold/supplied in the course of a business, and the buyer makes known to the seller their purpose for the goods (either expressly or impliedly) and reasonably relies on the seller's skill/knowledge, there is an implied term that the goods will be fit for that purpose.	Sale of goods. Supply of goods under a goods and services contract.
11 Where there is a sale/supply by description there is an implied term that the goods will correspond with that description.	Sale of goods. Supply of goods under a goods and services contract.
17 The seller has the right to sell or transfer the goods at the time when ownership of the goods is to be transferred.	Sale of goods. Supply of goods under a goods and services contract.
49 Where work or a service is done in the course of a business there is an implied term that it will be carried out with reasonable care and skill.	Goods and services and service contracts.
51 If a price for work or a service has not been fixed, there is an implied term that a reasonable sum will be charged.	Goods and services and service contracts.
52 Where work or a service is done in the course of a business and no time for performance has been agreed, it is implied that the work will be done within a reasonable time.	Goods and services and service contracts.

Examples

Situation	Term broken
Jenny decided to have a conservatory built at the back of her house and contracted with Windows Ltd for them to build it. Two days after the conservatory was completed, it became apparent that some of the double glazed window panels were defective and were getting misted up. When she pointed this out to Windows Ltd, they said it was not their fault as it was a manufacturing defect.	This is a goods and services contract within the CRA 2015 as made between a trader and consumer. There is a breach by Windows Ltd of the implied terms as to satisfactory quality and fitness for purpose – ss 9 and 10. Liability is strict, so it is no excuse that the fault is due to a manufacturing defect.
Patrick employed John, a local builder, to supply and lay a grey Indian stone patio at the back of his house. In the event John laid brown Indian stone and did not lay it properly as the surface was not level.	This is also a goods and services contract governed by the CRA 2015. Brown instead of grey stone is breach of an express term and also s 11 of the CRA 2015 (the implied term that goods will correspond with their description). In practice it would be better to sue for breach of s 11 (a statutory right). Not laying the patio properly would be breach of s 49 of the CRA 2015 – the implied term to exercise reasonable care and skill.

Consumers' rights to enforce terms about goods

These rights are set out in s 19 of the CRA 2015, and, broadly speaking, if the goods do not conform to the contract because of a breach of ss 9–11, the consumer has:

(a) the short-term right to reject and get a full refund (ss 20 and 22);

(b) the right to repair or replacement (if appropriate) (s 23); and

(c) the right to a price reduction or the final right to reject and get a partial refund to reflect the consumer's use of the goods (ss 20 and 24).

Basically, this is a pecking order of remedies. If the short-term right to reject has been lost, then consider whether it is appropriate/reasonable to get the goods repaired or replaced; if not, then the consumer may be entitled to an appropriate price reduction or to reject the goods and to get a partial refund of the price.

Note that a consumer's common law right to claim damages (see **Chapter 8**) is unaffected by the rights set out in s 19 of the CRA 2015. So if the remedies set out in s 19 do not fully compensate the buyer for losses suffered as a result of the breach damages may be awarded too.

Unless the parties have expressly agreed otherwise, the time limit for the short-term right to reject non-perishable goods is 30 days after they have been bought, delivered and, where appropriate, installed. With perishable goods, the time limit is no longer than the goods could reasonably be expected to last.

For the purposes of the other rights, if goods do not conform to the contract at any time within six months of the date of delivery, they will be taken as not having conformed to the contract on that day. The only exceptions to this are in relation to perishable goods and where it can be proved that the goods did conform to the contract on the day (but this may be very difficult to establish).

Consumers' rights to enforce terms about services/work

Very simply, s 54 of the CRA 2015 provides that where a service/work does not conform to the contract because of either breach of an express term relating to the performance of the service/work or breach of the implied term to exercise reasonable care and skill (s 49), the consumer has the right to require repeat performance (where reasonable) or to a price reduction.

In relation to a breach of the implied term as to performance within a reasonable time (s 52), the consumer simply has the right to an appropriate price reduction.

 Examples

Situation	Term broken	Remedy/remedies
Jenny decided to have a conservatory built at the back of her house and contracted with Windows Ltd for them to build it. Two days after the conservatory was completed, it became apparent that some of the double glazed window panels were defective and were getting misted up. When she pointed this out to Windows Ltd, they said it was not their fault as it was a manufacturing defect.	This is a goods and services contract within the CRA 2015 as made between a trader and consumer. There is a breach by Windows Ltd of the implied terms as to satisfactory quality and fitness for purpose – ss 9 and 10. Liability is strict, so it is no excuse that the fault is due to a manufacturing defect.	Exercise short-term right to reject the faulty window panels but might be more practical to go for replacement window panels. Repair or a price reduction would not seem to be appropriate or desirable.
Patrick employed John, a local builder, to supply and lay a grey Indian stone patio at the back of his house. In the event John laid brown Indian stone and did not lay it properly as the surface was not level.	This is also a goods and services contract governed by the CRA 2015. Brown instead of grey stone is breach of an express term and also s 11 of the CRA 2015 (the implied term that goods will correspond with their description). In practice it would be better to sue for breach of s 11 (a statutory right). Not laying the patio properly would be breach of s 49 of the CRA 2015 – the implied term to exercise reasonable care and skill.	Exercise the short-term right to reject but again might be more appropriate to claim replacement stones that conform to the contract description. Patrick could require repeat performance in preference to a price reduction (which is unlikely to be desirable).

Summary

Contracts contain both express and implied terms (**Figure 6.3**).

- Express terms may be incorporated in contracts in the following ways:
  - Signature (provided the clause is legible; not particularly onerous and not reasonably drawn to the other party's attention; and has not been misrepresented)
  - Reasonable notice before, or at the time of, the contract
  - A previous consistent course of dealing
- Terms are classified as either conditions, warranties or innominate terms.

- If a condition is breached prima facie the innocent party can terminate the future performance of the contract as well as claim damages.
- If a warranty is breached the only remedy is damages.
- With innominate terms the parties have to wait and see what the consequence of breach is. The innocent party will be entitled to terminate the contract only if the breach effectively deprives them of substantially the whole intended benefit.
- Terms may be implied:
  - by custom;
  - in fact, based on the presumed intention of the parties;
  - in law, where as a legal incident certain terms are implied into contracts of common occurrence such as employment contracts; and
  - by statute (eg the SGA 1979, which implies certain terms into business-to-business contracts for the sale of goods).

Figure 6.3 Contents of contracts

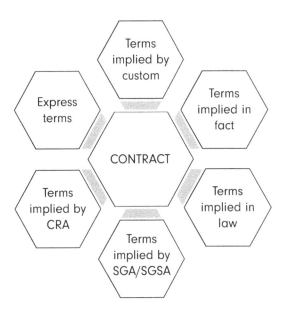

Sample questions

Question 1

A client, a private landlord, employed a builder to supply and fit a new kitchen in one of the properties she lets out. The agreed price was £10,000 payable on completion. Before the work was finished the client sacked the builder because his workmanship was substandard. The builder denies this allegation and has sued the client for loss of profit.

Which of the following statements best describes the client's legal position?

A If the builder had been in breach of the statutory implied term that the building work had to be performed with reasonable care and skill, the client was entitled to sack him.

B The client was not entitled to sack the builder because the statutory implied term that the building work had to be performed with reasonable care and skill is classified as a warranty.

C   Unless the builder had committed a very serious breach of the statutory implied term that the building work had to be carried out with reasonable care and skill, the client was wrong to dismiss him.

D   The term implied by statute that the building work had to be performed with reasonable care and skill imposes strict liability and so if the workmanship was in any way defective the client was justified in sacking the builder.

E   If the workmanship was substandard the builder had breached an implied condition of the contract and so the client had a choice whether to affirm the contract or dismiss the builder.

Answer

Statement C is correct as the term implied by s 13 of the SGSA 1982 is an innominate term. The term implied is that work/service in a business-to-business contract will be carried out with reasonable care and skill.

Statements A, B and E are wrong as the term implied by s 13 of the SGSA 1982 is innominate.

Statement D is wrong as the term implied by s 13 of the SGSA 1982 does not impose strict liability.

Question 2

A client employed an estate agent to sell his house. It was agreed that the estate agent would be paid 1% commission on the sale price of the property if the estate agent finds a buyer for it.

Which of following statements best describes the client's legal position?

A   The client may withdraw his house from the market without being liable to pay commission.

B   The client made an offer of a unilateral contract, which cannot be revoked once the estate agent has started to market the house.

C   The contract is one for work and materials and terms relating to both goods and services will be implied by statute.

D   The contract is a bilateral contract for the provision of a service, which must be carried out with reasonable care and skill.

E   If the client withdraws his house from the market the estate agent can sue him for breach of an implied promise to allow the estate agent the chance to earn commission.

Answer

Statement A is correct. The common intention of the parties must have been that the client should be able to withdraw the house from the market without liability for breach.

Statements B and E are wrong as it would not be implied (as it does not go without saying) that your client must keep his house on the market just so the estate agent can earn commission.

Statement C is wrong as the estate agent will simply be providing a service.

Statement D is wrong as it is a unilateral contract ie a promise in return for an act. The estate agent is not bound to find a buyer for the house and the client is only bound to pay commission *if* he does so.

Question 3

A client bought and paid for an exercise bicycle from a company for £500 (including free delivery). Two weeks after the bicycle had been delivered to the client's home, the client discovered it was inherently faulty; the pedals kept jamming. The client wants to reject the bicycle and get a full refund.

If the client decides to sue the company, which of the following statements describes the most likely outcome?

A   The company will have to repair or replace the defective bicycle as appropriate.

B   The client can reject the bicycle, get a refund plus any extra money it will cost to buy a similar bicycle elsewhere.

C   The client cannot reject the bicycle but will be entitled to a partial refund of the price to cover the cost of repair.

D   The client cannot reject the bicycle but the company must repair it without undue delay.

E   The client can reject the bicycle but will only get a partial refund to reflect the use he has had of the bicycle.

Answer

B is the correct statement. The company has breached the terms implied by ss 9 and 10 of the CRA 2015 (ie satisfactory quality and fitness for purpose) and liability is strict. The client could exercise the short-term right to reject (CRA 2015, ss 20 and 22) as the client has only had the bicycle two weeks ie less than 30 days. The client would be entitled to a full refund and to claim damages if it will cost more to buy a similar bicycle elsewhere.

A is wrong because the right to repair or replacement goods (CRA 2015, s 23) only applies when the short-term right to reject has been lost.

C and D are wrong as the client is still able to exercise the short-term right to reject.

E is wrong because if the client exercises the short-term right to reject the client will be entitled to a full refund notwithstanding two weeks' use of the bicycle.

7 Exemption Clauses

7.1	Introduction	64
7.2	Common law rules	64
7.3	Statutory controls	65
7.4	Exemption clauses and third parties	69

SQE1 syllabus

This chapter will enable you to achieve the SQE1 assessment specification in relation to functioning legal knowledge of the limitation and exclusion of liability.

Note that, for SQE1, candidates are not usually required to recall specific case names or cite statutory or regulatory authorities. Cases are provided for illustrative purposes only.

Learning outcomes

By the end of this chapter you will be able to apply relevant core legal principles and rules appropriately and effectively, at the level of a competent newly qualified solicitor in practice, to realistic client-based and ethical problems and situations in the following areas:

- advising on the incorporation and construction of exemption clauses;
- advising on the statutory controls of exemption clauses; and
- advising on the reasonableness test in the Unfair Contract Terms Act 1977.

Contract

7.1 Introduction

Commercial suppliers often include clauses in contracts to limit, or exclude, their liability for loss or damage in the event of failure to perform the contract properly (eg if goods are delivered late, or a service is performed badly).

One of the main problems with these clauses is that they are often hidden away in the supplier's written standard terms, often referred to as the 'small print'. Many buyers do not bother to read the small print before entering a contract (eg when you buy items on the internet, do you ever bother to read the seller's terms and conditions before 'accepting' them?). Buyers only tend to turn their attention to the small print if, and when, there is a problem with performance; so it is only then that they discover it contains exclusion clauses or other onerous terms.

Consequently, common law rules and statute have evolved to protect buyers from unfair contract terms, such as exclusion clauses.

7.2 Common law rules

The common law has developed two tests relating to exemption clauses, namely incorporation and construction.

The first test determines whether an exemption clause truly is part of the contract between the parties. The second one relates to the meaning – or, as lawyers put it, the construction – of the exemption clause, and asks, 'Does the clause exempt liability for the particular breach and loss suffered?'

7.2.1 Incorporation

We considered the various ways in which clauses may be incorporated into contracts in **Chapter 6**. As you may recall the three main ways are:

- Signature (provided the clause is legible; not particularly onerous and not reasonably drawn to the other party's attention; and has not been misrepresented)
- Reasonable notice, before or at the time of the contract, considering:
  - Contractual nature of the document (eg a quotation)
  - How onerous the term is (the more onerous a term, the more steps that need to be taken to bring it to the other party's attention)
  - Legibility
  - Position of the clause (eg hidden away in the small print)
  - Timing (notice must be given before, or at the time of, the contract)
- Previous consistent course of dealing (ie a lot of dealings on exactly the same terms)

7.2.2 Construction

The question here is whether the clause was intended to exclude or otherwise limit liability for the particular breach and loss that has occurred. The process of construction may be quite straightforward.

For example, a notice in a supermarket car park that reads 'Cars parked at owner's risk' is only purporting to exclude liability for damage caused to cars: it will not exempt the supermarket from being liable for personal injury or other loss or damage caused by the negligence of one of its employees.

Similarly, an exemption clause that excludes the claimant's right to treat the contract as *terminated* will not prevent the claimant from claiming *damages* for breach.

In both cases, it is quite clear what the wording of the exemption clause does and does not cover. These are clear cut cases.

But if there *is* any ambiguity or uncertainty about the meaning of a clause, the courts will apply the rule of construction known as the 'contra proferentem rule', ie the clause will be construed *against* the person seeking to rely on it. The idea is this: the defendant has contractually undertaken an obligation, and it is only fair that they should be liable for the performance of that obligation unless the contract clearly and unambiguously states otherwise.

 Examples

Clause	Facts
'The Company is not responsible for damage caused by fire to customers' cars on the premises.'	Claimant's car was being repaired at the defendants' garage when it was damaged by fire caused by the defendants' negligence.
Car insurance policy excluded liability for damage 'caused or arising whilst the car is conveying any load in excess of that which it was constructed for'.	At the time of the accident there were six people in a car with seating accommodation for only five.

In both cases the exemption clause was held not to cover the liability in question. In the first case the court said the clause was merely a 'warning' that the defendants would not be liable for accidental fire and in the second case the court held that the word 'load' covered only cases where there was a specified weight that must not be exceeded, as in the case of lorries or vans.

The first case in particular shows the difficulty that can occur in cases involving negligence. If a party wishes to exclude liability for negligence or lack of care, then the language of their exemption clause must make it very clear that they are not to be liable even in the event of their negligence or carelessness.

7.3 Statutory controls

The two main statutes that govern limitation and exclusion clauses are the Unfair Contract Terms Act (UCTA) 1977 and the CRA 2015. Very simply, UCTA 1977 governs exemption clauses in business-to-business contracts and CRA 2015 governs exemption clauses in business-to-consumer contracts.

7.3.1 Unfair Contract Terms Act 1977

The aim of UCTA 1977 is to restrict the effectiveness of certain types of exemption clauses.

Applying UCTA 1977 will give us one of three results (**Figure 7.1**):

(a) it *prevents* the defendant from excluding or restricting their liability by reference to the term (eg in relation to death/personal injury caused by negligence – UCTA 1977, s 2(1)) and the seller's implied undertaking as to title (ownership) of goods sold or transferred (UCTA 1977, s 6(1)(a) and s 7(3A)); or

(b) it has *no effect* on the term, and so the defendant can rely on the term (eg a clause in a freely negotiated contract that exempts liability for breach of an express term – UCTA 1977, s 3); or

(c) it subjects the term to a 'requirement of reasonableness'. This means that the defendant can rely on the term only if it satisfies this requirement. If it does not, UCTA 1977 will prevent the defendant from excluding or restricting their liability by reference to it. Indeed, if UCTA 1977 does apply, then, more often than not, it subjects the exemption clause to the requirement of reasonableness.

Figure 7.1   Application of Unfair Contract Terms Act 1977

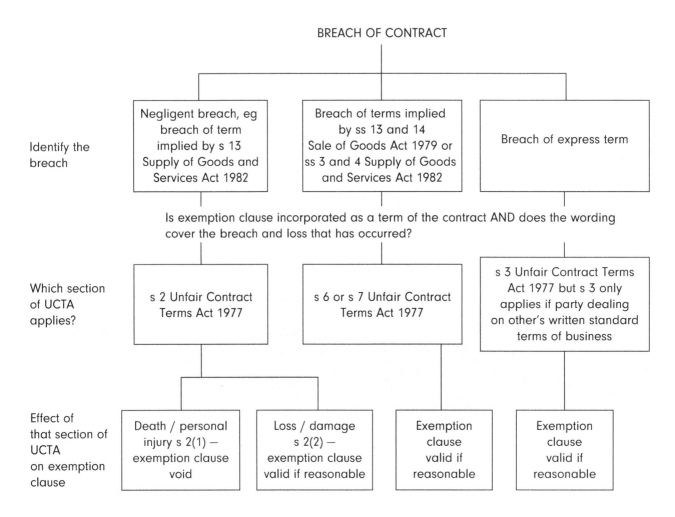

7.3.1.1 The reasonableness test

The reasonableness test applies to most exemption clauses in business-to-business contracts and in particular to clauses exempting liability for:

- loss or damage (other than death and personal injury) caused by negligence (including breach of the term implied by SGSA 1982, s 13) – UCTA 1977, s 2(2);

- breach of the statutory implied terms relating to goods – description, quality and fitness for purpose – UCTA 1977, ss 6 and 7 (s 6 applies to sale of goods contracts and s 7 applies to goods supplied under a work and materials contract); and

- breach of an express term contained in the standard written terms of the person seeking to exempt liability – UCTA 1977, s 3.

To satisfy the reasonableness test the clause must have been a fair and reasonable one to be included in the contract. And we judge that *at the time of the contract* by taking into account all the circumstances including what the parties knew or ought to have known at that point in time.

Examples

Situation	Clause more or less likely to be reasonable?
The seller is a large company that insists on selling goods on its own standard terms and conditions, which contain exemption clauses similar to those of other suppliers.	The buyer is in a weaker bargaining position than the seller, and the seller may be taking advantage of the buyer's position. That makes it *less* likely to pass the reasonableness test.
The seller agreed to reduce the price of goods if the buyer was prepared to accept the exemption clause.	The buyer has chosen to get the lower price in exchange for the exemption clause. It would be a touch harsh on the seller to deny them the benefit of the exemption clause, when in effect the seller has paid for the protection of the exemption clause by reducing the price. That all makes it *more* likely to pass the reasonableness test.
The exemption clause is set out in the small print at clause 76(3)(i)(d). Clause 76 is headed 'Other matters'.	Whether the customer knew – or even ought to have known – about the clause is relevant to determining its *reasonableness*. Here, the clause is buried in the small print and overall is less likely to be reasonable.
Experienced businessmen representing substantial companies enter into a freely negotiated contract including exemption clauses.	More likely to be reasonable. The courts have shown a marked reluctance to find clauses unreasonable where they have been agreed between substantial businesses.

UCTA 1977 itself provides for a number of factors (such as the above) to be considered in appropriate circumstances. These are set out in Sch 2 of the Act (see below). But, generally speaking, the courts will consider any relevant factor in deciding whether the clause was a fair and reasonable one. Such things as whether the risk was insurable, and the nature of the parties' dealings and negotiations, will almost invariably be relevant to an assessment of where the risks should fairly lie.

Schedule 2 guidelines

The Sch 2 guidelines say that the court should have regard to certain matters if they appear relevant. These include the following:

(a) The relative strength of the bargaining positions of the parties.

For example, if the bargaining positions of the parties are equal, it will be easier to show that the exemption clause is reasonable, whereas if a multinational corporation dealing with a small trader is purporting to exclude liability it may be regarded as unreasonable.

(b) Did the customer receive an inducement to agree to the exemption clause, or in accepting it did the customer have an opportunity to enter a similar contract with someone else, but without having to accept a similar exemption clause?

For example, if the customer could have gone elsewhere and avoided an exemption clause but chose not to do so, the court might feel that they had some good reason for accepting the contract with the clause and be reluctant to interfere with the agreement the parties had reached.

(c) Whether the customer knew, or ought reasonably to have known, of the existence and extent of the clause, taking into account any trade custom or previous dealings between the parties.

For example, if the clause is clearly worded and clearly set out in the document, the court might be encouraged to say that the clause is reasonable as the customer should have been aware of the existence and extent of the clause.

(d) Where the exemption clause will apply if a condition is not complied with, whether it was reasonable at the time of the contract to expect that compliance with the condition would be practicable.

For example, a clause that excludes all liability for defects in goods unless the defects are notified to the supplier within seven days of delivery would no doubt be unreasonable in relation to latent defects.

There are also additional guidelines in UCTA 1977 that apply to limitation clauses. If the court is trying to decide whether a limitation clause is reasonable, the court should also have regard to:

- the resources that the defendant could expect to be available to them for the purpose of meeting the liability should it arise; and
- how far it was open to the defendant to take out insurance cover.

Some important points to note about these guidelines are, first, they are only guidelines. The court has to consider and weigh up a range of matters. As a result, there are cases where it is impossible to say that one view is demonstrably wrong and the other demonstrably right.

Secondly, the guidelines are not meant to be a comprehensive set of relevant factors. Courts should consider *all* relevant factors, including the difficulty of the task. When a very difficult or dangerous undertaking is involved there may be a high risk of failure, which would certainly be a pointer towards the reasonableness of excluding liability as a condition of doing the work.

One final point to note is that UCTA 1977 makes it mandatory for the court to consider the guidelines in specified cases, eg the court must have regard to the guidelines in Sch 2 in cases involving the sale or supply of goods.

7.3.2 Consumer Rights Act 2015

As mentioned earlier, CRA 2015 basically governs exemption clauses in business-to-consumer contracts. Also, as the name of the Act suggests, most of the terms implied by CRA 2015 are effectively 'rights' because liability for breach cannot be excluded or limited by clauses in the contract.

7.3.2.1 Sales contracts

Section 31 of the CRA 2015 provides that liability for breach of s 9 (goods to be of satisfactory quality), s 10 (goods to be fit for particular purpose) and s 11 (goods to be as described) cannot be excluded or restricted. This includes preventing an obligation or duty arising in the first place.

So a term in a sales contract is not binding on the consumer to the extent that it would:

(a) exclude or restrict a right or remedy in respect of breach of ss 9–11;

(b) make such a right or remedy or its enforcement subject to a restrictive or onerous condition;

(c) allow a trader to put a person at a disadvantage as a result of pursuing such a right or remedy; or

(d) exclude or restrict rules of evidence or procedure.

Therefore, requirements for goods to be of satisfactory quality, fit for their particular purpose and as described are all non-excludable statutory rights that consumers should be able to enforce without restriction to attain the appropriate remedy.

7.3.2.2 Service contracts

Similarly, s 57 of the CRA 2015 effectively provides that a trader cannot exclude (compare restrict) liability for breach of s 49 (the implied term to perform a service with reasonable care and skill). This also includes preventing an obligation or duty arising in the first place.

To illustrate how a trader might do this, let us consider for a moment a domestic decorating contract. You would expect the decorator to use dust sheets etc to cover the carpet and furniture as part of their duty to exercise reasonable care and skill under s 49. It goes without saying. So if there was a clause in the contract that made protection of the carpets and furniture the householder's responsibility, the decorator would be redefining their implied contractual obligations; in other words, the decorator would not be liable in the first place, if they did not take reasonable care to protect the carpet etc.

Furthermore, a trader cannot restrict liability for breach of s 49 or, where they apply, ss 51 and 52 (reasonable price and reasonable time), if it would prevent the consumer in an appropriate case from getting a refund.

Finally, a trader cannot:

(a) exclude or restrict a right or remedy in respect of liability for breaches of ss 49–52;

(b) make such a right or remedy or its enforcement subject to a restrictive or onerous condition; or

(c) put a person at a disadvantage as a result of pursuing such a right or remedy, or exclude or restrict rules of evidence or procedure.

In this way, the statutory controls add to the common law rules of incorporation and construction (**Figure 7.2**).

Figure 7.2 Summary of the three 'hurdles' that exemption clauses need to clear

7.4 Exemption clauses and third parties

Sometimes an exemption clause may seek to protect someone who is not a party to the contract, and we shall now go on to consider the law on this.

The general rule is that an exemption clause in a contract cannot protect a third party, as the privity rule (considered in **Chapter 4**) provides that only a party can rely on a clause in a contract.

> *A case that illustrates this is* Adler v Dickson [1955] 1 QB 158. *In* Adler v Dickson *Mrs Adler was injured boarding a ship. Her contract was with the shipping company and contained an exemption clause. She sued the master and boatswain alleging negligence in not securing the gang plank. The court held that the master and boatswain were not protected by the exemption clause as they were not parties to the contract.*

A major exception to this general rule that exemption clauses do not protect third parties is contained in the C(RTP)A 1999 (see **Chapter 4**). Provided a third party is named in an exemption clause or identified as a member of a class entitled to benefit from it, the third party can rely on the exemption to the same extent as the relevant contracting party.

⭐ Example

Jordan took his taxi cab to Car Care Ltd to be serviced. When he drove the taxi away from Car Care Ltd, the brakes failed and the taxi crashed into a tree. The taxi was damaged and Jordan was injured. Jordan has now discovered that the reason the brakes failed was negligence on the part of George, a mechanic employed by Car Care Ltd.

Clauses in the contract between Jordan and Car Care Ltd provide:

> 8.1 Neither Car Care Ltd nor any of its employees will be liable for loss or damage to property howsoever caused (including negligence).
>
> 8.2 Neither Car Care Ltd nor any of its employees will be liable for personal injury, unless caused by negligence.

Statements	True or false?
Jordan could sue Car Care Ltd for breach of contract.	True. Car Care Ltd is in breach of the term implied by s 13 of the SGSA 1982, ie Car Care Ltd has not provided the service with reasonable care.
If clause 8.1 is found to be incorporated into the contract and reasonable, Car Care Ltd could rely on it to protect it from liability in respect of damage to the taxi.	True. Section 2(2) of the UCTA 1977.
If clause 8.2 is found to be incorporated into the contract and reasonable, Car Care Ltd could rely on it to protect it from liability in respect of the injury.	False. As a matter of construction, the clause does not cover injury. If it did, s 2(1) of the UCTA 1977 would apply – cannot exempt liability for death or injury caused by negligence.
Jordan could sue George for breach of contract.	False. There is no contract between them.
Jordan could sue George in the tort of negligence.	True.
If clause 8.1 is incorporated into the contract and reasonable, George could rely on it to avoid liability in respect of the taxi because of the C(RTP)A 1999.	True.
George cannot rely on the clauses as he is not named in the contract.	False. George does not have to be named – he is identified as a member of a class, ie employee.

Summary

- To be upheld, exemption clauses must clear three 'hurdles'. The first two 'hurdles' are the common law rules of incorporation and construction. An exemption clause must be incorporated as a term of the contract and as a matter of construction it must purport to exclude liability for the particular breach and loss. The last 'hurdle' is the relevant statutory control whether that be UCTA 1977 or CRA 2015.

- If UCTA 1977 applies the reasonableness test will usually be relevant. The only exceptions are where the clause purports to exclude negligence liability (including breach of the term implied by SGSA 1982, s 13) resulting in death or personal injury, or liability for breach of the seller's implied undertaking in contracts for the sale/supply of goods as to ownership of the goods; in these cases the exemption clause will be void (ineffective).
- Generally in business-to-consumer contracts a supplier cannot exclude liability for breach of the key terms implied into contracts for the sale and supply of goods and services. To that extent the implied terms are effectively 'consumer rights'.
- Third parties may rely on an exemption clause if they are named or otherwise identified as a member of a class intended to benefit from it.

Sample questions

Question 1

A client took his heavy goods vehicle (HGV) into the garage for a service. New brakes were fitted but as the client drove the HGV back to the depot the brakes failed. As a result the HGV was damaged and the client was injured. As yet the cause of the brake failure is unknown.

The contract with the garage does not contain any express terms about the quality of the new brakes or the level of service in fitting them but purports to exempt the garage from liability 'for any loss or damage caused by defective parts or workmanship howsoever caused'.

Which of the following statements best describes the client's potential legal position in relation to the garage and/or the employee who fitted the brakes?

- A If the brakes were inherently defective the garage will not be in breach of contract because there are no express terms promising that the brakes would be of a certain quality.
- B If the brakes were not fitted properly the client can sue either the garage or employee for breach of the statutory implied term to carry out work with reasonable care and skill.
- C If the client sues the garage for breach of contract, the garage will be liable for the personal injury but will not be liable for damage to the HGV if the exemption clause is reasonable.
- D If the client sues the garage for breach of the implied term to exercise reasonable care and skill the garage will be liable for damage to the HGV and the personal injury as the exemption clause does not specifically refer to negligence.
- E If the brakes were inherently defective and the garage is sued for breach of the implied terms as to quality and fitness the garage will be liable for the damage to the HGV and the personal injury caused.

Answer

The correct statement is C. Whatever the breach (SGSA 1982, s 4 or s 13) the exemption clause will be subject to the reasonableness test (UCTA 1977, s 7 or s 2(2)). The clause is not purporting to exclude liability for personal injury.

A is wrong. Notwithstanding that there were no express terms regarding the quality of the brakes fitted, terms as to quality and fitness fall to be implied under statute. The relevant statute would be the SGSA 1982. The contract was one for work and materials.

B is wrong as the client does not have a contract with the employee.

D is wrong. Although very clear words are needed to exclude liability for negligence, 'workmanship howsoever caused' is likely to cover it. The garage will be liable for the personal injury in any event as the clause is not purporting to exclude liability for it.

E is wrong. The garage will be liable for the injury as the clause is not purporting to exclude liability for that (contra proferentem rule). The garage will only be liable for the damage if the clause does not pass the reasonableness test.

Question 2

A client, a sole trader, ordered new machinery from a large company for use in their business and to be delivered on 14 December. The company was three months late delivering the machinery. The signed contract was made on the company's written standard terms, which included a clause stating that the company would not be liable for late delivery of the machinery.

Which of the following best describes the client's potential legal position in relation to the company?

- A   The exemption clause is part of a signed written contract. As a result, the company will not be liable for late delivery.
- B   The exemption clause may not be reasonable, in which case the company would be liable for breach.
- C   The exemption clause is valid at common law and so the company will not be liable for late delivery. The reasonableness or otherwise of the clause is irrelevant.
- D   The exemption clause is valid at common law and reasonable so the client can terminate the contract and claim damages.
- E   The exemption clause is valid at common law but automatically void under statute and the company would be liable for late delivery.

Answer

B best describes the client's legal position. The contract is on the seller's written standard terms, in which case s 3 of the UCTA 1977 will apply and the exemption clause will be valid if reasonable (so C and E are wrong). Due to all the circumstances including the apparent disparity in the bargaining positions of the parties the clause may well be deemed unreasonable.

A is wrong as the clause may be unreasonable on the facts.

D is wrong because *if* the clause was reasonable the company would not be liable for late delivery.

Question 3

A client bought a new computer from a commercial retailer for their personal use at home. Three weeks later the computer broke down due to an inherent manufacturing fault. When the client reported the problem the retailer denied liability on the basis it had effectively excluded liability: there was a clear notice at the payment point that said 'The Seller accepts no liability for defective goods unless the defect is reported within 7 days of purchase'.

Which of the following statements best describes the client's potential legal position in relation to the retailer?

A The retailer will not be in breach of the statutory implied term of satisfactory quality as it could not reasonably have known of the defect.

B The retailer would be liable for breach of the terms of quality and fitness implied by statute.

C The client will not be able to exercise the short-term right to reject the computer as the client will be deemed to have accepted it.

D The client may be entitled to reject the computer and get a refund; but they cannot require the retailer to repair or replace it free of charge.

E The retailer will not be liable for breach of any statutory implied terms as the fault was not reported within seven days of purchase.

Answer

The correct statement is B.

As the client bought the computer for their personal use from a trader the CRA 2015 will apply. Section 9 is the implied term regarding satisfactory quality and s 10 is fitness for purpose. Both terms will have been breached due to the inherent defect and liability cannot be excluded or restricted.

A is wrong as s 9 of the CRA 2015 imposes strict liability.

C is wrong as the short-term right to reject lasts for 30 days. Acceptance is a bar to rejecting goods under the SGA 1979.

D is wrong because the remedies of repair and replacement are available under the CRA 2015.

E is wrong because the terms implied by ss 9 and 10 of the CRA 2015 are non-excludable (CRA 2015, s 31) and so the retailer will be liable.

PART 3
REMEDIES

8 Damages

8.1	Introduction	78
8.2	Expectation and reliance loss	78
8.3	Types of loss recoverable	80
8.4	Remoteness of damage	80
8.5	Mitigation of loss	82
8.6	Quantification of damages	82
8.7	Specified damages and penalty clauses	83

SQE1 syllabus

This chapter will enable you to achieve the SQE1 assessment specification in relation to functioning legal knowledge of damages, which is the main remedy for breach of contract.

Note that, for SQE1, candidates are not usually required to recall specific case names or cite statutory or regulatory authorities. Cases are provided for illustrative purposes only.

Learning outcomes

By the end of this chapter you will be able to apply relevant core legal principles and rules appropriately and effectively, at the level of a competent newly qualified solicitor in practice, to realistic client-based and ethical problems and situations in the following areas:

- identifying recoverable types of loss;
- calculating the amount of damages; and
- advising on the limitations to recovery of damages.

8.1 Introduction

The idea of an award of damages is to provide compensation so far as money can do it for loss the claimant suffers as a result of a breach of contract. It is not generally to punish the defendant, nor to recoup from them any benefit they have obtained from breaching the contract.

So, if there is a breach but a claimant has not suffered any loss, a court may award so-called nominal damages – often a sum of £10 or the like. But this is only recognition of the fact that the contract has in fact been broken. What we are really interested in is what are called substantial damages. These are intended to compensate the claimant for loss suffered, and not just to acknowledge the fact that the contract has been broken.

It follows that the loss for which compensation is being claimed must have been caused by the particular breach of contract. For example, if a garage fitted defective brakes and you crashed your car, you would need to show that it was the defective brakes that caused the crash rather than, say, you driving recklessly. In contract, whether a particular breach has caused a loss is normally just an application of common sense.

8.2 Expectation and reliance loss

How do we set about identifying what someone's 'loss' is as a result of a breach of contract? The normal rule in contract is to compare the claimant's position after the breach, with where they would have been if the contract had been properly performed. The reason being that the breach has deprived them of the benefits they expected to obtain from the defendant performing the contract.

⭐ Examples

1. Ayesha sells a Ming vase to Barbara for £50,000. It is a term of the contract that the vase is Ming. In fact the vase turns out to be a copy worth £1,000. Had it actually been Ming it would have been worth £60,000.	The court is likely to award Barbara £59,000. If the contract had been properly performed, Barbara would have a Ming vase worth £60,000. In fact, she has a fake worth £1,000. She needs £59,000 so that she can buy an equivalent vase.
2. Carol agrees to buy goods from David at a price of £1,000, payment on delivery. Delivery to be on 1 October. David refuses to deliver. (In fact he had sold the goods to someone else for £2,000.) On 1 October Carol can buy similar goods elsewhere for £1,200.	The court is likely to award damages of £200. If the contract had been properly performed, Carol should have received the goods for £1,000. If she has to pay £1,200, she will have paid £200 more, so she needs this amount in damages. The fact that David makes a profit out of the breach is not relevant – the court will compensate Carol, not punish David.
3. Esher & Co orders goods from Fields plc at a price of £8,000 to be paid on delivery. Delivery to be 1 October. Fields plc tries to deliver on 1 October but Esher & Co refuses to accept the goods. Fields plc can sell elsewhere but only for £2,500.	The court is likely to award £5,500. If the contract had been properly performed, Fields plc would have received £8,000. Now the company can only sell for £2,500 – so it needs £5,500 to put it in the position it would have been in if the contract had been properly performed.

4. Jason, sole owner of a gardening business, agreed to cut down a tree in Carol's garden and remove all timber from the premises for £250. He agreed to do the work on 1 May. On 26 April Carol told Jason that she had changed her mind and no longer wanted him to cut down the tree. Jason could not find alternative work for 1 May. He tells you that he would have made a net profit of £220, taking into account the expenses he would have had to pay to do the job, including the fee to dispose of the timber.	The court is likely to award Jason £220. If the contract had been properly performed, Jason would have earned £250 altogether. However, in order to earn that sum, he would have had to pay out expenses amounting to £30, and these must therefore be deducted.
5. Smith is a manufacturer of cables. With his old machine, • he made £10,000 of cables per week, • he had costs of £5,000 per week (materials, labour and servicing) • giving him a profit of £5,000 per week. He recently bought a machine from Jones, which they calculated would enable him to: • make £10,000 worth of cables per week • with costs of £4,000 per week • giving him a profit of £6,000 per week. In the first three weeks of its operation, the machine only worked at 70% of its proper capacity, because of a fault (which Jones has now rectified). As a result, Smith could only make £7,000 worth of cables per week. However, his costs were only £3,000 per week, as he used fewer materials. What can Smith claim? £3,000?	Smith was £3,000 worse off using his new machine than if he had used his old one. But his complaint is not that he bought the new machine and now wishes he had not done so; his complaint is that the new machine did not work as well as it should have. What we need to find out is how much Smith has lost compared with his position if the new machine had been working properly from the start. So what about giving him £9,000? Well, the machine may have been operating at reduced capacity for a while, but he was still making £7,000 worth of cables per week. And it is true that over three weeks, he has made £9,000 worth fewer cables than he did before. But over those three weeks, he has also saved costs of £3,000. If you awarded Smith £9,000 damages, you would actually be making him better off than if the contract had been properly performed. You would be giving him £9,000 to compensate his loss of production, but also letting him keep his £3,000 saved costs. The object is merely compensation, so he cannot have £9,000. What he should get is £6,000. Why? Well, if the contract had been performed properly, he would have been able to make £9,000 worth more of cables, but would have incurred £3,000 more costs. Because of the breach, he is £6,000 worse off. Give him £6,000 and he is in the same financial position as he would have been if the contract had been properly performed. Put another way, Smith gets what he bargained for.

So the normal rule in contract is to look at the claimant's position 'as it is', and compare it with the position the claimant would have been in if the contract had been performed. Lawyers call this 'expectation loss' or 'loss of bargain' – because the claimant has lost the full benefit of the bargain they struck.

Occasionally, though, a claimant may decide not to claim for loss of bargain/loss of profits and instead just claim for expenses incurred because of reliance on the contract being performed. This is referred to as 'reliance loss'. The circumstances in which a party claims reliance loss may arise where the profits they hope will materialise from the contract are too speculative.

A case that illustrates this is Anglia Television v Reed *[1972] 1 QB 60 (CA). Anglia engaged the defendant, an actor, to play the leading role in the production of a play for television. The defendant later refused to carry on with the contract and Anglia was forced to abandon the production as it could not get a substitute. Anglia claimed as damages all of the expenditure that they had wasted on the production, which included such things as director's fees, designer's fees and stage manager's fees.*

The Court of Appeal awarded the wasted expenditure, which included expenditure that Anglia had incurred before entering into the contract with the defendant.

The reason Anglia TV did not claim damages on an expectation loss basis was because they did not know what profit (if any) they would have made if the contract had been properly performed by the defendant.

8.3 Types of loss recoverable

Some types of loss are very easy to translate into financial terms – eg the amount of lost profit or the amount of damage to property. These sorts of losses are called 'pecuniary losses' – they are the consequences of breach that can be 'put right' – remedied – by an award of damages. So, if you can establish that you would have made £6,000 more profit if the contract had not been broken, then £6,000 is obviously the right amount to award you.

On the other hand, things such as physical inconvenience, pain and suffering cannot be readily assessed in financial terms. These are known as 'non-pecuniary losses'. Here, the link between the loss to be compensated and the amount of the compensation is in some sense arbitrary, though obviously the law has got rules to ensure you get more for a broken arm than, say, a broken fingernail.

Non-pecuniary losses are comparatively unusual in contract. Some of them can only be claimed in limited circumstances. For instance, whilst damages for disappointment or mental distress can be awarded for breach of contract, this will normally only happen if one of the objects of the contract was to provide pleasure or peace of mind. Holiday contracts and weddings provide good examples of where disappointment caused by breach of contract can be claimed.

 A case that illustrates this is Jarvis v Swans Tours *[1973] 1 QB 233 (CA). The defendants, a firm of travel agents, advertised a 'houseparty' holiday in Switzerland. The claimant, Mr Jarvis, booked a two weeks' holiday with the defendants and paid £63.45. The holiday was a catalogue of disasters. There was supposed to be a 'houseparty' but there were only 13 guests there during the first week and none during the second – apart from Mr Jarvis. The holiday failed to comply with the description in the brochure in numerous other respects too and all in all Mr Jarvis had a pretty miserable holiday and brought an action for breach of contract. The Court of Appeal held that he was entitled to damages for his loss of enjoyment and awarded him the sum of £125.*

8.4 Remoteness of damage

It is a fair enough starting point in awarding damages to work on the basis that the defendant should compensate the claimant for all the losses suffered. But it is not hard to think of circumstances where the losses the claimant suffered may have been very improbable, or unpredictable, in which case it would be unfair to make the defendant responsible for all of them.

Example

Rudi sold his old camera in the paper for £100 and gave the buyer a one-year guarantee. If it broke a month later, Rudi might reasonably expect to pay for a repair. But what if unbeknown to Rudi the buyer had contracted to take photographs at a wedding and because the camera broke lost £2,000 profit on the deal. Should Rudi be liable for that additional unanticipated loss?

Lawyers call this issue 'remoteness' of loss. The cost of repairing the camera if it breaks would not be too remote for the buyer to claim it. On the other hand, the loss of profit from the wedding photograph contract would be too remote and the buyer would have to put up with that loss, and could not recover it.

Remoteness of loss hinges on whether a particular type of loss would have been in the reasonable contemplation of the parties at the time of the contract as being a likely consequence of the breach (see **Figure 8.1**). If a certain loss would be an inevitable or natural consequence of breach then the parties will be deemed to have had it in their reasonable contemplation at the time of the contract. For any other type of loss it will depend on what the defendant actually knew at the time of the contract. Did they know of special circumstances that meant the particular loss would be a likely consequence of breach? In the sale of the defective camera example above, the reason the £2,000 loss of profit would be too remote is that the buyer did not tell Rudi about the wedding contract before buying the camera.

Figure 8.1 Remoteness of loss in damages claims

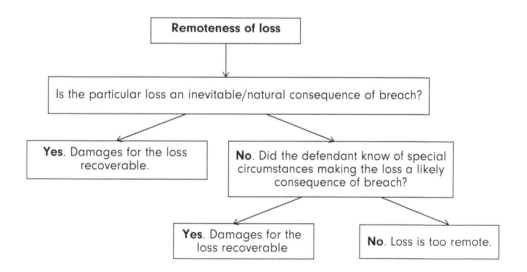

As long as the particular type of loss is not too remote then the extent of the loss is irrelevant. So if physical injury or damage is within the contemplation of the parties, recovery is not limited because the degree of physical injury or damage could not have been anticipated.

This point is illustrated by Parsons (Livestock) Ltd v Uttley Ingham [1978] 1 QB 791. *The claimants were pig farmers. They bought a hopper from the defendants for storage of pig food. The defendants agreed to erect the hopper but forgot to unseal the ventilator at the top of the hopper. As a result, pig food stored in the hopper became mouldy and, after eating it, many of the pigs contracted a rare infection and died. The claimants brought an action for damages for breach of contract. The Court of Appeal held that because illness of the pigs would have been within the reasonable contemplation of the parties at the time of the contract as being a likely consequence of the breach, the death of the pigs was not too remote.*

8.5 Mitigation of loss

To mitigate a loss is simply to take steps to reduce the amount of it. Not surprisingly, if there has been a breach of contract, the law does not allow the claimant simply to sit back, watch the losses add up, and then pass the cost onto the defendant by claiming damages. The claimant has to take *reasonable* steps to mitigate the loss caused by the breach.

Examples

Situation	Mitigation
Sheila is dismissed from her job as a dental assistant in breach of contract.	Sheila should look for suitable alternative employment as a dental assistant.
In breach of contract, Ellery refuses to deliver goods to Nasser.	Nasser should go into the marketplace straight away and try to buy similar goods elsewhere.
Arjuna tries to deliver goods to Pauline, but in breach of contract Pauline refuses to accept delivery.	Arjuna should go into the marketplace straight away and try to sell the goods elsewhere.
Hugh agrees to paint all the rooms in Elnora's house. He paints the kitchen, but then abandons the job because he can earn more money elsewhere.	Elnora should look for someone else to finish the painting at a reasonable price. She should obtain two or three comparable quotations and accept the cheapest.

Claimants will not be allowed to claim for any part of the damage that was due to their failure to take reasonable steps to mitigate their loss. This might seem to impose an undue burden on the claimant; but there are a number of ways in which the law is not overly harsh on claimants:

- First, the burden of showing that the claimant has failed to mitigate their loss is placed upon the defendant and the defendant may find this difficult.
- Secondly, a claimant who has acted reasonably can claim for their loss, even if their reasonable attempts to mitigate have failed to reduce their loss, or even increased it. What steps count as reasonable is a question of fact for the court to decide.

8.6 Quantification of damages

Imagine we act for a claimant who has suffered a loss, eg received defective goods or a poor service. We decide that they are claiming compensation for a recoverable type of loss that is not too remote. So, what happens next? We need to 'quantify' or measure it, so that the loss is, as it were, translated into financial terms.

This is often a fairly straightforward task. For example, if work is defective the normal measure of loss is the cost of putting it right – the cost of reinstatement, or so-called 'cost of cure'. With defective goods, on the other hand, the starting point for the law is the difference in value between the goods (as they are) and the goods as they were expected to be.

But things are not always quite so straightforward, and sometimes it can be hard to work out what would count as 'putting the claimant in the same position as they would have been in if the contract had been properly performed'.

This is illustrated by Ruxley Electronics v Forsyth *[1996] AC 344.*

Ruxley agreed to build a swimming pool for Mr Forsyth in his garden. Mr Forsyth stipulated that the deep end of the pool should be 7 feet 6 inches deep. In the event it was only 6 feet 9 inches deep. It was established there was no difference in value, but it was going to cost £21,560 to rectify the problem.

The question before the House of Lords was whether Mr Forsyth should get nothing (representing the difference in value), £21,560 (representing the cost of cure) or a sum somewhere between those two figures. The original trial judge had awarded Mr Forsyth £2,500.

Whilst cost of cure (here £21,560) is the normal measure in cases of defective work, the House of Lords did not consider it should be used where it was unreasonable in relation to the benefit to be obtained. So the House of Lords reinstated the original trial judge's award of £2,500 as representing the true loss suffered by Mr Forsyth; namely that his personal preference for a deeper pool had not been satisfied. The House of Lords referred to this loss as 'loss of amenity' and the 'consumer surplus'.

One significant aspect of the case was that it was all about a swimming pool – something meant to provide pleasure and amenity. So the loss of amenity/consumer surplus could be viewed as his 'true' loss. If the contract had been for a more mundane construction, Mr Forsyth might have received nothing, on the basis that there would have been no loss of value or amenity and that curing the defect would have been unreasonable. Conversely, if the depth of the swimming pool had been critical for some reason and consequently may well have been rebuilt, the full cost of cure (ie £21,560) may have been awarded.

8.7 Specified damages and penalty clauses

Bringing a claim for damages can be costly and time-consuming, and so the parties may put a clause in their contract stating the amount of compensation to be paid if there is a particular breach. This tends to be quite common in commercial contracts. Stating in the contract the exact amount of compensation that will be paid provides certainty. The parties can see by looking at the contract the amount that will be paid or received in the event of a particular breach. If the contract is broken and both parties are willing to abide by the clause, the cost of going to court will be avoided. Also, depending on how the clause is drafted, the innocent party may not have to prove the extent of their loss, only that the breach has occurred.

8.7.1 The distinction between a specified (or liquidated) damages clause and a penalty clause

If both parties are happy to abide by the clause, the issue will not come before the court. However, one party might want to avoid the operation of the clause and if this happens the court will then have to decide whether the clause is a specified damages clause or a penalty clause.

A specified damages clause has been defined as a genuine attempt to pre-estimate the loss that is likely to be caused by the breach. Such a clause is binding and the sum specified is the amount that will be paid regardless of the actual loss that the claimant has suffered. The usual rules of measure of damages, remoteness and mitigation do not apply and the claimant may receive more or less than the loss actually suffered. The crucial figure is the amount of compensation stated in the clause. (Note that a specified damages clause is often referred to as a 'liquidated damages' clause.)

A penalty may be defined as an attempt to put pressure on a party to perform the contract because the sum stipulated is extravagant or otherwise disproportionately high. A penalty is unenforceable. Where the clause is a penalty, the court is free to assess damages in the usual way and the usual principles of measure of damages, remoteness and mitigation will apply.

Contract

8.7.2 How does the court decide whether the clause is a specified damages clause or a penalty clause?

In Cavendish Square Holding BV v Makdessi; ParkingEye Ltd v Beavis [2015] 3 WLR 1373 the Supreme Court said that the penalty rule was concerned with two questions. The first was the circumstances in which the rule was engaged. The Supreme Court said that a provision could not be a penalty unless it provided an exorbitant alternative to ordinary damages. The second question was concerned with whether the clause was penal and not whether it was a pre-estimate of loss (which had traditionally been one of the main guidelines). The fact that the clause was not a genuine pre-estimate of loss did not necessarily mean it was penal. The Supreme Court said that the real test of a penalty clause turned on whether the means by which the contracting party's conduct was to be influenced were unconscionable or extravagant. This was formulated as a test of whether the clause imposed a detriment on the contract-breaker out of all proportion to any legitimate interest of the innocent party in the enforcement of the contract.

In ParkingEye Ltd v Beavis Mr Beavis had parked in a car park operated for the landowner by ParkingEye. There were prominent notices in the car park that said parking was limited to two hours and that a fee of £85 would be imposed for overstaying. Mr Beavis parked for three hours and ParkingEye demanded payment of the £85 fee. Mr Beavis argued it was unenforceable as a penalty. The Supreme Court dismissed his appeal. Although ParkingEye was not liable to suffer loss as a result of overstaying motorists, it had a legitimate interest that involved receiving income to meet the legitimate costs of running the car parking scheme. This in itself was a legitimate way for the landowner to regulate the efficient use of the car park.

The rules on types of loss recoverable, remoteness of damage, mitigation of loss and specified damages all work to limit the amount of damages awarded (**Figure 8.2**).

Figure 8.2 Limitations on awards of damages

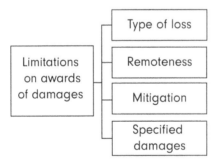

Summary

- Damages are available for all breaches of contract. If there has been no loss the claimant will be awarded only nominal damages.

- The aim of damages is loss of expectation, ie to put the claimant, as far as money can do it, in the position the claimant expected to be in if the contract had been properly performed.

- Most types of loss are recoverable, although damages for distress/disappointment only tend to be awarded where the main purpose of the contract was to provide pleasure or peace of mind.

- The type of loss must not be too remote, ie it must be a natural consequence of the breach or otherwise the defendant must have known at the time of the contract of special circumstances making the loss a likely consequence of the breach.
- The usual measures of loss are difference in value and cost of cure. However, damages have been awarded for loss of amenity where there was no difference in value and the cost of cure was deemed out of all proportion to the loss sustained.
- Claimants must take reasonable steps to mitigate their loss.
- Parties to commercial contracts may agree in advance the amount of damages payable in the event of a particular breach. Specified (liquidated) damages clauses are enforceable and the specified amount is what the claimant will be awarded whatever their actual loss. Penalty clauses, on the other hand, are unenforceable and damages will be assessed in the usual way.

Sample questions

Question 1

A client, a professional tennis player, employed a company to construct a tennis court for practice purposes. When the tennis court was finished the client discovered the length of the court was 1cm too short.

In a claim for breach of contract, which of the following measures of damages is a court most likely to award?

A Consumer surplus

B Difference in value

C Cost of cure

D Distress and disappointment

E Nominal

Answer

Statement C is correct. As the client is a professional tennis player, the dimensions of the court would be critical. The loss is not just a personal preference that has not been satisfied (so A is wrong) and the client is likely to use any damages awarded to rebuild the tennis court. Nominal damages will only be awarded where there is no sustainable loss as a result of the breach and so E is wrong. Damages for distress only tend to be awarded where the main purpose of the contract is pleasure/enjoyment and that is not the case here, so D is wrong. Statement B is wrong as there may be no, or little, difference in value.

Question 2

A client agreed to buy goods at a price of £1,000, payment on delivery. Delivery to be on 1 October. The seller refused to deliver because the seller knew he could sell the goods to someone else for £2,300. On 1 October the client could buy similar goods elsewhere for £1,200.

In a claim for breach of contract, which of the following most likely reflects the amount of damages the client would be awarded by a court?

A The client will be awarded £1,300 by way of damages.

B The client will be awarded £200 plus damages for the distress involved in sourcing the goods elsewhere.

C   The client will be awarded £1,000 damages on a reliance loss basis.

D   On 1 October the client could buy similar goods elsewhere and so will be awarded £200 by way of damages.

E   The client will be awarded £2,300 as the aim of damages is to punish the defaulting party for the breach.

Answer

Statement D is correct. The client will be expected to mitigate their loss by going out into the marketplace on the date of breach and buying similar goods elsewhere. £200 would represent the client's loss of bargain.

Statements A and E are wrong as the aim of damages in contract is to compensate the innocent party and not to punish the defaulting party.

Statement B is wrong as damages for distress/disappointment are normally confined to contracts where the main purpose was to have peace of mind, eg a holiday contract.

Statement C is wrong as £1,000 would over compensate the client for loss of bargain.

Question 3

A client, a joiner, decided to set up his own business. He contracted with a builder to convert his garage into a workshop. The price was £10,000 and the work was to be completed by 1 March. However, problems with labour meant that the builder did not finish the work until 1 June.

Which of the following best describes what the client would be able to recover by way of damages?

A   The loss of profit from cancelled joinery contracts for the period between March and June.

B   All loss of profit from cancelled joinery contracts between March and June including loss of profit on a special contract he had with a stately home to make bespoke shelving for its library.

C   Loss of profit from cancelled joinery contracts between March and June and the mental distress caused by the delay in starting the business.

D   The expenditure your client wasted between March and June because expectation loss would be too speculative.

E   Nominal damages in recognition that the contract had been breached and the client had suffered loss as a direct result.

Answer

Statement A is correct. Ordinary loss of profit would be within the reasonable contemplation of the parties as being a likely consequence of breach and so would not be too remote.

Loss of profit on the special contract would be too remote unless the builder had been told about it in advance. That is why B is wrong.

C is wrong because damages for distress are typically only awarded where the purpose of the contract was enjoyment, eg in relation to holidays.

D is wrong as expectation loss (ie loss of profit) is unlikely to be too speculative.

Nominal damages are only awarded where a claimant cannot establish a loss as a result of the breach and that is why E is wrong.

9 Equitable and Other Remedies

9.1	Remedies that make the defendant perform the contract	88
9.2	Restitution	89
9.3	Guarantees	92
9.4	Indemnities	93

SQE1 syllabus

This chapter will enable you to achieve the SQE1 assessment specification in relation to functioning legal knowledge of equitable and other remedies for breach of contract and in restitution.

Note that, for SQE1, candidates are not usually required to recall specific case names or cite statutory or regulatory authorities. Cases are provided for illustrative purposes only.

Learning outcomes

By the end of this chapter you will be able to apply relevant core legal principles and rules appropriately and effectively, at the level of a competent newly qualified solicitor in practice, to realistic client-based and ethical problems and situations in the following areas:

- suing for the price or for a reasonable sum for goods/work supplied;
- obtaining a court order to compel a party to perform a contractual obligation or otherwise to stop a breach;
- advising on recovery of sums paid under a contract;
- advising on damages awarded on a restitutionary basis; and
- advising on guarantees and indemnities.

9.1 Remedies that make the defendant perform the contract

You know from previous chapters that damages is the main remedy for breach and that in certain circumstances the innocent party may also be entitled to terminate the future performance of the contract. Now we are going to look at some of the other remedies – those that actually make the defendant do what they agreed to do.

9.1.1 Action for an agreed sum

Actions for an agreed sum are sometimes called actions in debt or actions for the price. An action for an agreed sum is simply suing for a fixed amount of money that is owed – normally the price of goods or services supplied under a contract. It is a much more direct remedy than a claim for damages. Money has to be owed and the date for payment must have fallen due; but once a claimant can establish their right to the money, they can claim it (plus accrued interest for late payment). Issues such as proving loss and showing that it is not too remote drop out of the picture.

9.1.2 Specific performance

Specific performance is an equitable remedy. The idea here is that the claimant is asking the court, not for compensation, but for an order requiring actual performance; in other words, making the defendant do what they agreed to do. Normally this relates to doing things other than merely paying money.

Specific performance is not an 'alternative' remedy to damages. Specific performance is generally only available if damages are not an adequate remedy eg in relation to purchases of land.

⭐ Example

Claire has exchanged contracts to buy number 21, Acacia Avenue; but the seller has now changed his mind and is refusing to transfer it. Claire could seek damages if she has suffered loss – and then she could go and buy somewhere else to live. But even if Claire could get damages, the law would accept that damages would not be an adequate remedy: Claire did not want a house like 21 Acacia Avenue; Claire wanted 21 Acacia Avenue itself. So instead of damages Claire could get a court order requiring the seller to transfer the house to her.

Specific performance is not uncommon in contracts for the sale of land. Contrast that with sales of goods, where you cannot generally get specific performance – if a seller refuses to supply particular goods the buyer can claim damages and use the compensation to buy goods elsewhere that are just the same.

Also, specific performance will not usually be granted for contracts involving services such as an employment contract. The reason for this restriction is that such contracts depend on a certain amount of trust and confidence. If the relationship between the parties has broken down, it would be inappropriate to force them to work together.

Finally, as specific performance is an equitable remedy it is not available 'as of right' – it is at the discretion of the court. It will only be awarded when it is just and equitable to do so. The court will consider whether the claimant has acted equitably and will also look at whether the order would cause disproportionate hardship to the defendant.

9.1.3 Injunction

Like specific performance, an injunction is an equitable remedy. So it is only available at the discretion of the court and will only be awarded where damages would be inadequate.

However, whereas specific performance is used to make the defendant do what they have agreed to do, injunctions are more commonly used to restrain the defendant from doing what they have agreed not to do.

 Example

Reya agreed with the buyer of her hairdressing business that she would not set up another hairdresser's in the same village. The buyer might seek an injunction to restrain Reya if she tried to set one up. The injunction would be making Reya perform the contract by enforcing her promise not to set up another hairdresser's in the same village.

An injunction will not be granted, though, if the effect would be to compel the defendant to do acts that they could not be ordered to do by specific performance (eg the courts will not order an injunction that would effectively force an employee to work for a particular employer).

 This is illustrated by the case Page One Records v Britton *[1968] WLR 157, the claimant was the manager of a pop group, 'The Troggs'. The group had appointed the claimant as their manager for a period of five years and in their contract they had agreed not to engage any other person, firm or corporation to act as managers or agents or to act themselves in such capacity. The group dismissed the claimant as their manager. The claimant applied for an injunction to prevent the group employing another person to act as manager.*

The court refused to grant the injunction because if the group could not employ someone else, in practice this meant it would have to employ the claimant. Pop groups need managers. The court said it would be wrong to put pressure on the defendants in this way as the manager had duties of a personal and fiduciary nature to perform and the defendants had lost confidence in him.

9.2 Restitution

A claim in restitution may arise in a number of different situations – not just where there has been a breach of contract. Indeed, it may arise where no contract has come into existence at all. The general idea behind a restitutionary remedy is to prevent one party being unjustly enriched at the expense of the other party. However, it is important to note that a claim in restitution is not available in every case where there has been an element of unjust enrichment.

We are going to consider the restitution claims that may arise:

- where money has been paid by one party under the contract and there has been a total failure of consideration; and
- where one party has done work for the other, or supplied goods to the other, and wants to be compensated for the work done or goods delivered.

9.2.1 Recovery of money paid where there has been a total failure of consideration

If one party (the payer) has paid money to the other (the payee) under a contract, the payer can bring an action in restitution to recover the money if the payee is in breach and there has been a *total* failure of the consideration. A *total* failure of consideration is where the payee has not done any part of what they were supposed to do under the contract.

Examples

Situation	Total failure of consideration?
1. Shakira has paid £500 in advance for goods. The seller has agreed to deliver them.	A total failure of consideration would arise if the seller refuses to deliver the goods – for example if they know they can sell the goods for more money to someone else.
2. Bill has paid £800 in advance to get his house painted. The painter is supposed to start work next week.	There will be a total failure of consideration if the painter does not turn up to paint Bill's house.

In both of the above situations the payer will have received nothing at all for their money and so could bring a claim in restitution to recover the money. So in situation 1 Shakira could bring a claim in restitution and recover the £500. If she can buy similar goods for £500 or less, she will not need any other remedy. If she has to pay more, though, then she will need to bring a damages action either as well as, or instead of, restitution.

Similarly, in situation 2 Bill could bring a claim in restitution and recover the £800. If Bill could then get his house painted by someone else for £800, or less, he will not need any other remedy. But, if Bill has to pay more than £800 then he will need to bring a damages action.

Note that in situation 2 if the painter had started the job and then abandoned it, this would not amount to total failure of consideration. So Bill's only remedy would be damages for the amount he has to pay a new painter to finish off the work.

9.2.2 Compensation for work done or goods supplied

Two examples where this claim might be relevant are:

- where the contract has been broken; and
- where a contract was never formed.

9.2.2.1 The contract has been broken

Where one party has supplied goods or done work and then the other party breaches the contract, the party supplying the goods or doing the work may be able to bring a claim in restitution for a reasonable sum for the work done or goods supplied. This would be as an alternative to a claim for damages. The supplier has a choice – claim a reasonable sum or damages (ie net loss of profit on the project).

Example

Gavin agrees to build a garage for Ray. Gavin does some work and then Ray tells him to stop as he has changed his mind. He no longer wants the garage. Ray is in breach of contract.

Gavin can sue for damages or he can bring a claim in restitution. If a claim is made in restitution then Gavin will receive what is called a 'quantum meruit' ie a reasonable sum for what he did.

9.2.2.2 A contract was never formed

In some cases a party may do work for someone before a contract has been finalised. This sometimes happens with building work, where the negotiations between the parties may be complex and time-consuming but there is a desire to start the work as soon as possible. If a contract is ultimately not formed (eg because the negotiations break down) the building contractor would be entitled to a reasonable sum for the work they had done.

 A case that illustrates this is British Steel Corp v Cleveland Bridge and Engineering Co Ltd *[1984] 1 All ER 504. The claimants were iron and steel manufacturers. The defendants asked the claimants to produce a variety of steel nodes for a construction project they were engaged in. The parties had not finalised the contract but the defendants asked the claimants to start manufacturing the nodes straight away. The claimants prepared the nodes and delivered them to the defendants. The parties were unable to agree on some key terms of the contract. The court held that no contract had been formed, as the parties were still negotiating and had not reached agreement. However, the claimants were entitled to recover a reasonable sum for the work they had done.*

9.2.3 Restitutionary damages

As you may recall from the last chapter, the traditional purpose of an award of damages in contract is to compensate the claimant for the loss they have suffered as a result of the defendant's breach. Sometimes this is the expectation measure, sometimes it is the reliance loss measure – but, either way, its purpose is compensatory.

However, a line of cases has considered an award of remedies based, not on loss to the claimant, but on the gains made by the defendant. This feature also takes such awards outside the strict principles of restitution, which, as we have just seen, comes to the aid of a claimant when the defendant has made gains at the *expense* of the claimant. Here we are looking at gains made that do not – or, at least, do not *necessarily* – reflect the loss to the claimant.

 The first example of this approach we will look at is the exceptional case of Attorney-General v Blake *[2001] 1 AC 268. Blake was a notorious traitor. He was employed as a member of the secret service for 17 years from 1944. In 1951 he became an agent for the Soviet Union and disclosed valuable secret information. In 1961 he pleaded guilty to five charges of unlawfully communicating information and was sentenced to 42 years' imprisonment. In 1966 he escaped and fled to Moscow and then in 1989 wrote his autobiography. Blake entered into a publishing contract under which he would be paid £150,000 in advances against royalties. Plainly, had Blake not been an infamous spy who had also dramatically escaped from prison, his autobiography would not have commanded payments of this order. Certain parts of the book related to his activities as a secret intelligence officer; however, the information was no longer confidential, nor was its disclosure damaging to the public interest. So the money owed to Blake did not represent any loss to the Crown: it simply represented the benefit to Blake of the breach of his undertaking.*

The case was decided on the basis that, even though the Crown had suffered no financial loss as a result of the publication of the book, it should receive the benefit of the profits from its publication.

An account of profits for misuse of confidential information would be a perfectly normal remedy for breach of fiduciary duty. The problem was that Blake had long since ceased to be employed by the Crown, quite apart from the fact that the material in his book was no longer confidential. The argument that Blake still owed fiduciary duties was therefore rejected.

Nevertheless, it was held that an account of the wrongdoer's profits was appropriate in these exceptional circumstances where it was a just response to the breach of contract.

But does that leave us with a stark choice between compensation for financial loss, in the vast majority of cases, and an account of profits only in truly exceptional cases? Or does the claimant have another recourse somewhere in the middle? Something that is an award of damages, rather than an account of profits, but that is not simply based on loss suffered by the claimant?

The answer appears to be a cautious yes; and the term for it is restitutionary damages. It may also arise, as in the case below, where the claimant may suffer no discernible financial loss other than the opportunity to negotiate a release fee and where it would be unfair to allow the defendant to take the full benefit of their breach of contract.

 A case that illustrates this is Wrotham Park Estate v Parkside Homes *[1974] 1 WLR 798. Parkside Homes had acquired a plot of land. The land was subject to a restrictive covenant, which purported to restrict further building without the consent of Wrotham Park Estate, the owners of the land that had the benefit of the covenant.*

Parkside Homes nevertheless built on the land, and made a handsome profit in the process. When Wrotham Park Estate discovered the breach it sought a mandatory injunction ordering Parkside Homes to effectively demolish the development. A mandatory injunction is an extreme remedy and necessarily only awarded in exceptional circumstances. The development had caused no diminution in the value of the land owned by Wrotham Park Estate and to that extent no discernible financial loss. But Wrotham Park Estate had nevertheless lost the chance to negotiate a fee for relaxing the restrictive covenant.

The judge awarded damages to Wrotham Park Estate in substitution for the mandatory injunction that he was being asked to grant. He awarded a sum of five per cent of the developer's profit, being:

> ... such a sum of money as might reasonably have been demanded by the claimants from Parkside as a quid pro quo for relaxing the covenants.

So the damages in Wrotham Park were to compensate the claimant for the notional loss of the opportunity to bargain where that was the only loss.

The Supreme Court subsequently referred to such damages as 'negotiating damages' and made it clear that they should not be awarded where the claimant had suffered clear financial loss as a result of the breach, even if that loss would be difficult to calculate. In other words negotiating damages should not be awarded as an alternative to conventional damages – only where the only loss is the opportunity to negotiate a release fee.

Now we are going to look at ways in which a non-defaulting party may be able to claim against a third party in the event of breach by either suing on a guarantee or claiming an indemnity.

9.3 Guarantees

A contract of guarantee is a contract under which one person (the guarantor) guarantees that *if* another person (the debtor) does not pay back money owed then the guarantor will pay the money instead. For example a parent might guarantee a child's overdraft so that the bank will agree to lend money to the child under the overdraft facility.

So the essence of a contract of guarantee is that the guarantor agrees to discharge the debt, not in any event, but only if the debtor defaults. In other words, it is a secondary obligation to pay if, and only if, the debtor does not pay the money owed.

Contracts of guarantee must be 'evidenced in writing'. If not, they will be void and completely ineffective. 'Evidenced in writing' essentially means that although the contract itself need not be a written one, there must be some written evidence of the transaction. The evidence must have existed before the creditor seeks to enforce the contract and it must be signed by the guarantor. The note need not have been created for the specific purpose of enforcing the contract and may comprise a series of documents linked by reference.

9.4 Indemnities

An indemnity, on the other hand, creates a primary obligation. It is effectively where one party promises to reimburse pound-for-pound the other party in respect of a particular loss arising under the contract. As indemnities are primary obligations they do not have to be evidenced in writing.

Indemnities are often required by commercial buyers in relation to business acquisitions and purchases of land where there is a known specific liability/loss that the buyer will be taking on board. For example, a potential buyer of land discovers it is contaminated and that cleaning it up will cost £100,000. The buyer could negotiate an appropriate price reduction or alternatively seek an indemnity for £100,000. A price reduction would effectively solve the problem. An indemnity solves the problem provided the seller reimburses £100,000 as and when required to do so.

In **Chapter 6** we briefly looked at express 'warranties' in sale and purchase agreements of businesses. The purpose of such warranties is to allocate unknown risks (such as the risk of third party litigation) to the seller; whereas the purpose of indemnities is to allocate known liabilities/losses to the seller.

The practical difference between guarantees (as secondary obligations) and indemnities (as primary obligations) is illustrated below (**Figure 9.1**).

Figure 9.1   Guarantee and indemnity

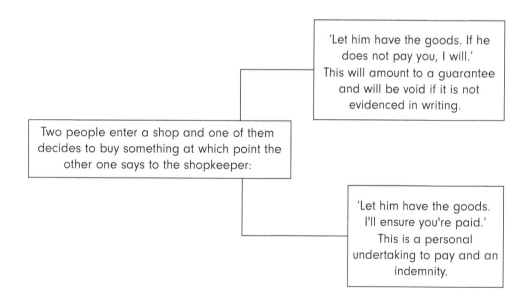

Contract

Summary

- The main remedies that make a defendant perform the contract are:
  - Action for an agreed sum (which is a straightforward debt action)
  - Specific performance
  - Injunction
- Specific performance and injunctions are both equitable remedies. They are awarded at the discretion of the court when an award of damages would be inadequate.
- The aim of restitution is to stop one party being unjustly enriched at the expense of the other. Examples include:
  - recovery of money paid where there has been a *total* failure of consideration;
  - claim for a reasonable sum (as an alternative to damages) for goods or services supplied; and
  - claim for a reasonable sum for work done where a contract is never formed.
- A claimant will only be awarded an account of profit in exceptional circumstances.
- A claimant may be awarded a sum as negotiating damages where the only loss is the opportunity to negotiate a release fee.
- A guarantee is a secondary obligation to pay *if* the debtor defaults. Guarantees must be evidenced in writing.
- An indemnity is a primary obligation to pay for a known loss/liability. Indemnities do not have to be evidenced in writing.

Sample questions

Question 1

A client contracted to sell a consignment of tracksuits for £10,000, payment to be within 10 days of delivery. The signed contract included the following term: 'Time for payment shall be of the essence' ie a condition of the contract. The client delivered the tracksuits a month ago but has still not been paid for them.

What is the most appropriate remedy for the client?

A   Specific performance

B   Injunction

C   Damages

D   Action for the agreed sum

E   Termination

Answer

Statement D is correct. As a fixed amount of money is being claimed, action for an agreed sum (ie the money owed) is the most appropriate remedy. Action for an agreed sum is a debt action.

A and B are wrong as monetary compensation will be adequate.

C is wrong. Damages are subject to limitations such as remoteness and mitigation. When a fixed sum is owed and claimed there are no such issues.

E is wrong because although 'Time for payment shall be of the essence' means it is a condition of the contract it would be too late for our client to terminate. The goods have been delivered and so there is no future performance to terminate.

Question 2

A company ('the retailer') entered into a contract with another company ('the supplier') to buy 30,000 flat-pack boxes at a price of £60,000. The retailer paid £20,000 in advance. When delivered, the boxes were defective and the supplier was unable to supply replacement boxes. The retailer rejected the boxes and did not pay the balance of the purchase price. To avoid incurring further losses, the retailer obtained replacement boxes from another supplier for £70,000.

Ignoring interest, what sum can the retailer properly claim against the supplier?

- A £70,000
- B £10,000
- C £30,000
- D £20,000
- E £60,000

Answer

C is correct. The retailer paid £20,000 in advance to the supplier. The supplier gave nothing in return for that – there was a total failure of consideration and so the retailer is entitled to be reimbursed £20,000 in restitution. In addition it has cost the retailer an extra £10,000 to buy similar goods elsewhere and so the retailer would be able to claim that sum as loss of expectation damages (**Chapter 8**). The retailer took reasonable steps to mitigate its loss.

A and E are wrong as the retailer would have made a windfall profit as a result of the breach.

B is wrong because it does not take account of £20,000 paid in advance for which the retailer received nothing in return.

D is wrong as it ignores the extra money the retailer had to pay to buy replacement goods elsewhere.

Question 3

A client used to own a business. When the client sold the business the sale agreement included a restrictive covenant not to compete with the business nor to solicit customers. Unbeknown to the buyer the client had already set up a rival business and the client began operating in competition and poaching customers. As a result the buyer lost a considerable amount of business. The buyer is now suing the client for negotiating damages in relation to breach of the restrictive covenant.

Which of the following statements best describes whether, or not, the buyer will be successful?

- A Yes, because the buyer lost the opportunity to negotiate a fee for relaxing the restrictive covenant and there was no other loss.
- B Yes, because the buyer lost the opportunity to negotiate a release fee and it would be unfair to allow the client to benefit from breaching the restrictive covenant.
- C Yes, because the buyer lost the chance to negotiate a release fee and the client made profit at the expense of the buyer.

D   No, because it would be impossible for the court to know what release fee, if any, would have been negotiated.

E   No, because the buyer suffered an ascertainable financial loss other than the chance to negotiate a release fee.

Answer

The correct statement is E. Negotiating damages will only be awarded where there is no financial loss other than the chance to negotiate a release fee. Here there was loss of business, which could be assessed albeit with difficulty.

A, B and C are wrong. Negotiating damages will only be awarded where there is no financial loss other than the chance to negotiate a release fee. Here there was clear loss of business.

D is wrong because in appropriate circumstances a court will award a reasonable sum based on a hypothetical negotiation.

PART 4
TERMINATION

10 Termination

10.1	Termination	100
10.2	Frustration	101
10.3	Discharge by performance	106

SQE1 syllabus

This chapter will enable you to achieve the SQE1 assessment specification in relation to functioning legal knowledge concerned with the different ways in which contracts may be terminated.

Note that, for SQE1, candidates are not usually required to recall specific case names or cite statutory or regulatory authorities. Cases are provided for illustrative purposes only.

Learning outcomes

By the end of this chapter you will be able to apply relevant core legal principles and rules appropriately and effectively, at the level of a competent newly qualified solicitor in practice, to realistic client-based and ethical problems and situations in the following areas:

- advising on when a party may be entitled to terminate the future performance of a contract for breach;
- advising on when a contract will be terminated by frustration and the effects of frustration; and
- identifying the rights and remedies of parties where performance of the contract is not complete and precise.

Contract

10.1 Termination

As you will appreciate from your reading in **Chapter 6**, one of the rights that an innocent party might have when there has been a breach of contract is the right to terminate the future performance of the contract. This right arises in two main circumstances: where there is a breach of condition (a particularly important term of the contract), and where there is a very serious breach of a term classed as an innominate term (see **Figure 10.1**). These are called repudiatory breaches – breaches that allow the non-defaulting party to treat the breach as having brought the contract to an end. Generally, the innocent party will have a choice:

- affirm the contract (ie treat the contract as ongoing); or
- discharge the contract.

So the breach per se does not terminate the contract automatically. It is up to the innocent party whether, or not, to treat the contract as at an end. But if they affirm the contract, they cannot then change their mind. Affirmation is a bar to terminating a contract.

Figure 10.1 Consequences of breach of contract – summary

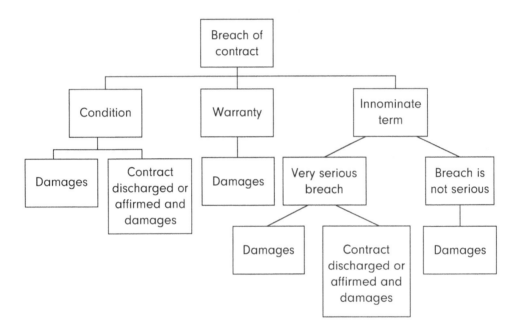

⭐ Example

Barot has engaged Attwal to build a house for her. Attwal has to carry out four stages of building, and Barot has agreed to pay for each stage in advance.

Barot pays the price for Stage 1 and Attwal completes Stage 1. Barot pays for Stage 2 and Attwal completes it. Barot pays for Stage 3, but then something goes badly wrong and Attwal breaches a condition of Stage 3.

Barot has the choice whether to treat the contract as terminated. She does not have to. She could affirm the contract and limit herself to a claim for damages for the breach. But if she does treat the contract as at an end then both parties are discharged from future performance of the contract. Barot does not have to pay any more but, equally, Attwal does not have to do any more building work.

Furthermore, if the breach of contract causes Barot any loss, she can sue for damages. For example, if it will cost her more than the outstanding payment for Stage 4 (the money she has saved to get the work completed) she is entitled to the excess as damages – though, as we have seen, she has to mitigate (take reasonable steps to reduce) her loss. For example, she would be expected to get a few quotes to complete the work from reputable builders and then accept the cheapest.

It is important to note that termination only operates to discharge parties from future contractual obligations: if there are none (eg because the contract has been performed), termination will be impossible. (Note: the rights and remedies for breach of contracts for the sale of goods are governed by the SGA 1979 and the CRA 2015 – see **Chapter 6**).

10.2 Frustration

Very occasionally the law excuses a party for non-performance; for example where a party can no longer perform a contractual obligation due to an unforeseen event beyond its control. So instead of the party being held liable for what has happened the contract is automatically brought to an end; both parties are excused from future performance; and the law determines how any losses should be borne by the parties. This is known as the doctrine of frustration – something out-of-the-ordinary has frustrated the intentions of the parties.

Frustration, then, is something that in practice is almost invariably used by the parties' practitioners as a defence to an allegation of breach of contract (**Figure 10.2**).

Figure 10.2   Consequences of non-performance

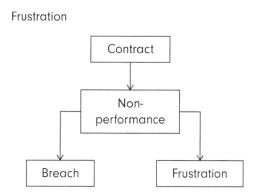

10.2.1   What constitutes frustration

Frustration only operates in limited circumstances. The supervening event or changes of circumstances must:

- make performance of the contract impossible, or radically different;
- be something beyond the ordinary risks that the parties can be treated as having taken on board when entering into their contract (ie something unexpected); and
- be something that was beyond the control of either party.

So where an unforeseen event occurs after the contract was formed, then generally if the parties are not at fault and such an event renders the performance of the contract very different, or even impossible to perform, a contract will be terminated by frustration. It is an exception to the general rule that requires complete performance of obligations to avoid being in breach of contract. We will consider the doctrine of complete performance at **10.3** below.

10.2.1.1 'Radically different'

Most of the cases that have considered frustration have been placed into convenient categories of circumstances that render performance of the contract 'radically different'. These categories include:

(a) Government intervention

(b) Unavailability of a specific person crucial to the contract

(c) Illegality

(d) Destruction of the subject matter

(e) Non-occurrence of a fundamental event

But in all cases it will be a question of degree.

 Examples

Situation	Frustrated – reason
Shahid agrees to hire the local community centre for 1 June so his amateur dramatic group can perform a play. Before 1 June someone breaks into the centre and starts a fire. The centre is completely destroyed.	The subject matter of the contract (the centre) is accidentally destroyed so it is impossible to perform the contract.
Shirjel has agreed to write a book for Bharat. The book must be completed in six months' time. Shirjel writes a couple of chapters but then falls ill. He will not be able to work for at least a year.	Shirjel is not going to be able to complete the book in six months' time because of his illness. The contract is impossible to perform. Note: Shirjel was vital to performance of the contract.
Someone hires a room for two days (not the nights) for the sole purpose of viewing the coronation procession of Edward VII. The procession is cancelled due to the illness of the King.	The whole purpose for hiring the room had been to watch the procession and that is no longer possible.

Situation	Not frustrated – reason
10 year lease of a warehouse. For 18 months of the 10 year term the local authority closes the street giving the only access to the warehouse.	Whilst frustration may apply to leases of land, here the relative length of the interruption would not be not sufficiently grave to amount to a frustrating event.
Sheila enters into a contract with Beautiful Interiors Ltd to have her house decorated. Mike, an employee of Beautiful Interiors, works on her house for a couple of days but then goes down with flu and is replaced by Phil, another employee. Sheila is looking for an excuse to end the contract as she would like to finish the decorating herself with the help of friends.	The contract has not become impossible to perform or radically different. Beautiful Interiors can still do the work by using Phil rather than Mike. Sheila makes her contract with Beautiful Interiors, and the identity of the employee who will do the work is not important so long as one of their employees can do it.
Someone agrees to hire a ship for two days to take people out to view the royal Naval Review and for a day's cruise round the fleet. The Naval Review is cancelled due to the King's illness.	The royal Naval Review had not been the sole purpose of the contract. A day's cruise round the fleet is still possible and so performance has not become radically different.

One of the tricky areas to deal with is delay. Delay is not a category of frustrating event itself, as not every case of delay will frustrate the contract. In fact, a delay is more likely to mean that a party is in breach of contract. For example, if it is a term of the contract that the seller will deliver goods on 3 March and they do not do so, they are likely to be in breach of an express term of the contract and frustration would not apply. When deciding if delay frustrates the contract, relevant factors include:

- whether there are contract provisions for the consequences of delay;
- the likely length of delay relative to the duration of the contract;
- any time set in the contract for the obligations to be performed; and
- whether the performance resumed is radically different from the contract.

In the case of Metropolitan Water Board v Dick Kerr *[1918] AC 119, there was a clause in the contract to build a reservoir dealing with the possibility of an extension of time, in the case of delay. However, the court decided that the wording of the clause was meant to cover temporary delays and not an interruption of such character and duration that it fundamentally changed the conditions of the contract. The interruption was the First World War, and so could not really be assessed as a temporary delay. Such an interruption could not have been in the contemplation of the parties at the time the contract was made. As a matter of construction, the delay clause did not cover the situation that had arisen. The delay was such that the contract, if resumed, would be radically different from the contract the parties had originally made. Needless to say, the court held that the contract had been frustrated.*

It can sometimes be difficult to distinguish situations where delay frustrates the contract, because the contract becomes impossible, or radically different to perform, from situations where the contract merely becomes more difficult to perform or less profitable.

For example, the closure of the Suez Canal in 1956 led to many voyages being re-routed and the new voyages were longer and more expensive. The courts were reluctant to say that the contracts were frustrated unless a route via the Suez Canal had been specified in the contract; or a precise delivery date had been agreed; or the goods or value of the goods would have been adversely affected by the longer voyage.

Similarly, a 14-month delay in completing a building contract due to labour shortages was held not to have frustrated the contract. The court decided the building contract had just become more expensive and difficult to perform; it had not become radically different. Furthermore it was noted that the parties could have foreseen the cause of the delay (ie a shortage of labour) and so should have provided for it in the contract.

10.2.1.2 Something unexpected

It is important, when considering the event that may have caused frustration, to decide whether the parties could have foreseen the event. If the reason a party cannot perform the contract is due to some entirely predictable common event, then they will not generally be able to plead the doctrine of frustration. It is essentially for this reason that the defence would not be available if, say, machine parts do not arrive on time because of a road closure. A road closure is exactly the sort of risk that you can be taken to have in mind when entering into a contract for the delivery of goods.

Given the difficulty of identifying the precise limits of the law of frustration, and the fact that it must involve the occurrence of unexpected or unusual things, parties are often well advised to 'make provision for the unexpected' in their contracts.

As a result, most commercial contracts do make express provision to excuse parties from performance in the event of exceptional circumstances. They want to know where they stand, and what the risks are, not just in the ordinary course but in the event of exceptional occurrences. This helps, also, to cut down cost and litigation risks.

Once the contract makes provision for an event, it ceases to be something unexpected that is radically different from that which was undertaken by the contract; far from it: now the situation becomes one that is governed by the contract.

This means that where the parties have included a 'force majeure' clause governing a situation there is no room, or need, for the doctrine of frustration. The defendant's defence to non-performance now arises because it was agreed that the defendant need not perform in the specified circumstances.

Key points to note are:

- Illegality can never be provided for in the contract.
- As force majeure clauses effectively excuse a party from non-performance in specified circumstances they will be governed by s 3 of the UCTA 1977 and as such will have to satisfy the reasonableness test in order to be upheld (see **Chapter 7**).

10.2.1.3 Something beyond the control of either party

The fact that the supervening event or change of circumstances must be beyond the control of either party means that if it arises because of the fault or choice of the party alleging frustration, then that party will not be successful in defending an action for breach. In essence, the law takes the view that you should not be excused from what is your own fault.

 This is illustrated by The Super Servant Two *[1990] 1 Lloyd's Rep 1. The defendants agreed to transport the claimants' drilling rig from Japan to Rotterdam. The contract said the rig was to be carried using a 'transportation unit' defined as meaning Super Servant One or Super Servant Two. The defendants intended to use Super Servant Two but it sank before the date due for delivery. The defendants had entered into other contracts that they could only perform using Super Servant One and so two weeks after the sinking they informed the claimants that they would not be able to transport the rig. The Court of Appeal decided the contract had not been frustrated. What had happened was 'self-induced'. It was the defendants' decision to use Super Servant One for other contracts that had made performance of their contract with the claimant impossible. The impossibility of performance resulted from their own act and the choice they had made.*

10.2.2 Consequences of frustration

The future performance of the contract is terminated automatically as a matter of law. Therefore, both parties are released from all future obligations (ie obligations arising after the frustrating event) and neither party will be in breach of contract in respect of the frustrating event.

Note that discharge of the contract happens as a matter of law – the non-defaulting party does not have a choice whether, or not, to terminate the contract.

As well as bringing the contract to an end, it may be that one party has already paid money to the other or has incurred expenses in performing the contract, or has received a benefit under the contract.

The Law Reform (Frustrated Contracts) Act (LR(FC)A) 1943 lays down a complex set of rules governing the consequences of frustrating events for many types of contract, insofar as they relate to acts carried out, expenses incurred and obligations performed up until the point of the frustrating event. Section 1(2) contains three key points:

- Money paid before the event can be recovered.
- Money that should have been paid before the event need not be paid.

- At the court's discretion, expenses incurred by the payee can be recovered out of the total sums paid/payable before the event.

Section 1(2) deals with payments already made, or payments that should have been made but had not been made, before the frustrating event. Pre-payments can be returned. Also, money that should have been paid before the event need not be paid. But note also, that there is a *very wide discretion* afforded to the court to allow a payee to recover expenses out of the total money paid *and* payable before the frustrating event. If the expenses incurred are less than this total pot, then they can only recover the amount of expenses incurred.

Also note that, under s 1(3) of the LR(FC)A 1943, if one party has conferred a valuable benefit on the other party before the frustrating event, then the court may order a just sum to be paid by the recipient for that benefit. What is a just sum will depend on all the circumstances including the effect the frustrating event may have had on the benefit and any sum forfeited by the benefitting party under s 1(2) of the Act.

To appreciate how the common law and LR(FC)A 1943 operate in practice when a contract has been frustrated we are now going to consider a particular set of facts.

 Example

> Moira agrees to hire a boat from Jane for six weeks beginning on 1 August. Moira pays a £200 deposit and agrees to pay a further £400 on 15 July and the balance of £2,400 on 1 August. They agree that Jane will install some extra bunks. Jane has spent £800 installing the bunks when a fire destroys the boat on 16 July. Moira has not yet paid the £400 due on 15 July.
>
> Assume that the contract has been frustrated.
>
> 1. Moira does not have to pay the balance of £2,400. Frustration of the contract discharges future obligations.
>
> 2. Section 1(2) says that money paid before the frustrating event can be recovered and money payable before the frustrating event need not be paid. So Moira could recover her £200 deposit and need not pay the £400 (but this is subject to any award that the court makes for Jane's expenses (see below)).
>
> 3. Under s 1(2) the maximum the court can award for expenses incurred by the payee is a sum equal to the total paid and payable before the frustrating event or the amount of the expenses incurred (whichever is the lower sum). In this situation, the total money paid and payable before the frustrating event was £600 (ie the £200 deposit and the £400 due on the 15 July); whereas £800 had been spent by Jane (the payee) in performance of the contract. Therefore Jane could be awarded a maximum of £600 under s 1(2) and so would not be compensated in full.
>
>   The court has a broad discretion when it is contemplating an award for expenses under s 1(2). Its task is to do justice and it is not obliged to award the maximum amount.
>
> 4. Jane has done some work installing extra bunks in the boat. This would constitute a valuable benefit under s 1(3) but, as the frustrating event completely wiped out the work Jane had done before Moira could benefit from it, a 'just sum' might be nil.
>
>   If the fire had destroyed the boat on 8 August, Moira would have had use of the boat for one week and a court may decide that this amounts to a valuable benefit. The court would have to identify and value the benefit taking into account any expenses incurred by Moira including any money that Moira has to pay Jane under s 1(2). Having done this, the court would then have to decide on a just sum (if any) that Moira should pay. The court could have regard to the consideration (ie the amount Moira agreed to pay for the hire).

10.2.3 Frustration – summary

If an unforeseen supervening event occurs that was beyond the control of either party and made performance of the contract impossible, or otherwise radically different, the parties are discharged from their future obligations and the LR(FC)A 1943 determines how any losses should be borne by them (see **Figure 10.3**).

Figure 10.3 Frustration – summary

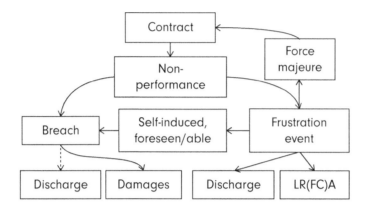

If a supervening event/change of circumstances falls outside the doctrine of frustration it is a breach of a contract, and/or is governed by the contract itself. As to whether the matter is governed effectively by a force majeure clause is a matter of construction of the contract itself. In the majority of commercial contracts, the parties make express provision for what is to happen and this is mainly why there are so few decided cases that have been brought before the courts under the 1943 Act.

10.3 Discharge by performance

The general rule is that performance of contractual obligations must be precise and exact. This is known as the doctrine of complete performance. If one party has to pay only after the other has performed their obligations under the contract, then if performance is not precise and exact, the payer does not have to pay any part of the price (although they will not be able to recover money already paid unless there has been a total failure of the consideration – see **Chapter 9**).

10.3.1 Exceptions

This doctrine could produce unfair results if applied in all circumstances and so there are exceptions. If an exception applies then some payment (albeit not the price) can be recovered, even though the contractual obligations have not been performed precisely and exactly.

The exceptions are:

(a) Divisible obligations
(b) Substantial performance

(c) Wrongful prevention

(d) Voluntary acceptance of part performance

10.3.1.1 Divisible obligations

Contractual obligations are divisible if the parties have agreed specific payments for each distinct part or stage of the contract. Each part or stage is then treated like a separate contract and so once it has been completed the contractor is entitled to be paid in full for it.

 Example

Brooks agrees to decorate some rooms in Sarah's house. It is agreed that he will be paid £200 for painting the kitchen, £400 for the dining room and £300 for a bedroom, payment to be made as each room is completed. He paints the kitchen and dining room and starts painting the bedroom, but then abandons the job for a more lucrative project.

Brooks would be entitled to be paid for decorating the kitchen and dining room, which he completed. He would not be entitled to any money for the work he had done on the bedroom.

10.3.1.2 Substantial performance

If a contractor has *completed* the agreed work but it is *slightly* defective they may not be entitled to the price, but they will be entitled to the price less the cost of putting right the defect. What constitutes work being slightly defective? As a general rule, as long as the cost of rectifying the problem is not more than 1/14 of the contract price a court is likely to accept that the work has been substantially performed.

 Example

Benjamin built a small extension to Michael's restaurant. The contract price was £10,000, payment on completion. Michael has discovered some minor defects, caused by faulty workmanship that will cost £100 to put right, and is refusing to pay Benjamin any more money.

Benjamin finished the work and it is slightly defective. He has substantially performed the contract and so will be entitled to £10,000 less £100 ie £9,900.

10.3.1.3 Wrongful prevention

If a party is wrongfully prevented from completing their contractual obligations they will be entitled to either damages or a reasonable sum in restitution for what has already been done. You considered damages and restitution in **Chapters 8** and **9** respectively. Also remember from **Chapter 6** and **10.1** above that it is only in very limited circumstances that a non-defaulting party may be justified in terminating the future performance of a contract, ie where there has been a repudiatory breach (breach of a condition or otherwise a very serious breach of an innominate term).

The term implied by s 13 of the SGSA 1982 into business-to-business contracts that service/work will be carried out with reasonable care and skill is an innominate term (see **Chapter 7**) and it is in relation to breach of this term that problems may arise. How bad does the work have to be before the employer is justified in terminating the contract? If the employer terminates in circumstances falling short of a serious enough breach, then that will be wrongful prevention and a repudiatory breach by the employer.

Examples

Situation	Wrongful prevention – so entitled to some payment?
Vince agrees to cut down the five trees in Eleanor's garden for £900, payment on completion. He cuts down two trees but then Eleanor says that she has changed her mind and she tells him to stop work.	Yes. She has breached the contract by telling him to stop. Vince will be entitled to his net loss of profit by way of damages or otherwise a reasonable sum for what he has done.
Wessex Builders Ltd agreed to build an extension to Sonia's cafe for £10,000 payment on completion. Half way through the project Sonia dismissed the builders because the work was very seriously defective.	No. The builders have committed a very serious breach of the term implied by s 13 of the SGSA 1982 to exercise reasonable care and skill. So Sonia was justified in dismissing them. Sonia will have got the work done for nothing.

Note in the second example above, if the work had not effectively deprived Sonia of the whole benefit she expected to receive under the contract then it would have been wrongful prevention.

10.3.1.4 Voluntary acceptance of part performance

Where a supplier of goods or services partly performs their contractual obligations and the other party *voluntarily* accepts the partial performance then the supplier is entitled to a reasonable sum for what they have done. Note, however, that the non-defaulting party must have a genuine choice whether, or not, to accept the part performance. If they have no choice (eg because the supplier built something on the non-defaulting party's land and then abandoned the job) the non-defaulting party will not have to pay anything for what was done.

This is illustrated by Sumpter v Hedges [1898] 1 QB 673. In that case a builder agreed to construct two houses and a stable on the defendant's land for £565. However, he abandoned the project after completing £333 worth of work. The defendant had to complete the work himself and he used materials left behind by the builder. The builder claimed a reasonable sum for work done and materials supplied. The claim for the work failed as the defendant had no choice but to accept what had been done. However, the defendant did have a choice whether, or not, to use the materials that had been left behind and so was ordered to pay a reasonable sum for those.

See **Figure 10.4** for a quick overview of the exceptions to the doctrine of complete performance.

Figure 10.4 Exceptions to the doctrine of complete performance – summary

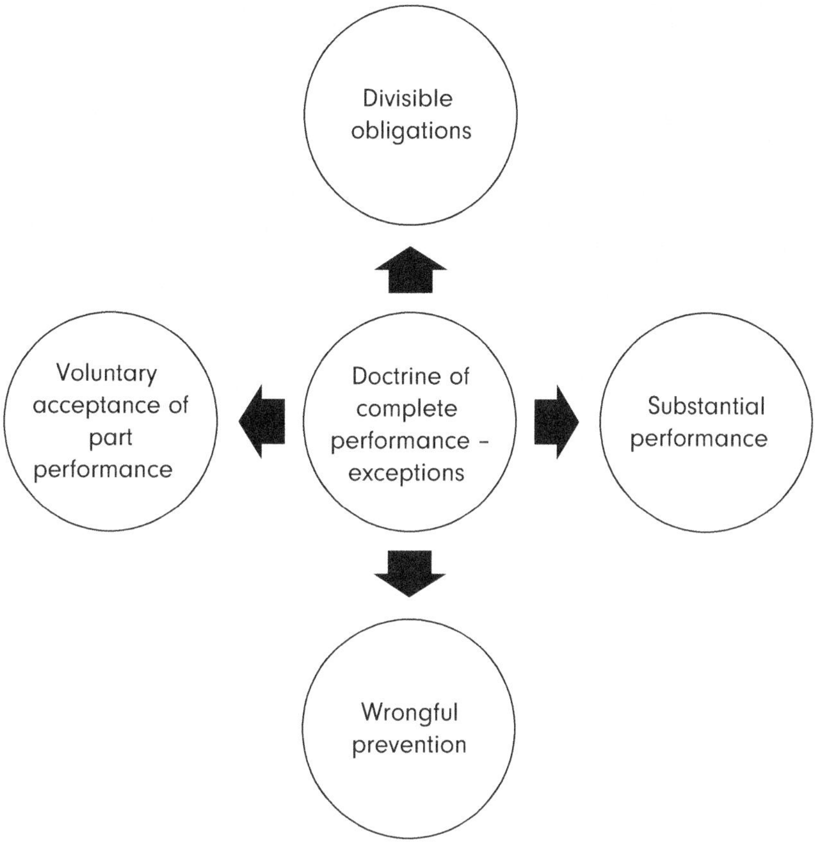

```
                    Divisible
                    obligations
                        ▲
                        │
  Voluntary        Doctrine of
  acceptance of ◄── complete ──► Substantial
  part              performance -   performance
  performance       exceptions
                        │
                        ▼
                    Wrongful
                    prevention
```

Summary

- Contracts may be terminated in the following ways:
  - Discharge following a repudiatory breach
  - Frustration
  - By performance
- Where there has been a repudiatory breach of contract the innocent party has a choice whether to affirm or discharge the contract.
- A supervening event or change of circumstances will frustrate a contract if it:
  - renders performance impossible or radically different;
  - was unexpected; and
  - occurred without fault.
- Frustration automatically terminates a contract. Both parties are relieved from future obligations and neither party will be in breach in relation to what gave rise to the frustrating event/ change of circumstances.
- The LR(FC)A 1943 provides for what should happen in relation to money paid and payable prior to frustration and also in respect of any valuable benefit conferred prior to the frustrating event/change of circumstances.

- Most commercial contracts contain a 'force majeure' clause, which provides for what should happen in exceptional circumstances. Force majeure clauses will be upheld provided they satisfy the reasonableness test in the UCTA 1977. If there is a valid force majeure clause the contract will not be frustrated.
- Under the doctrine of complete performance a supplier is not entitled to the price unless and until performance is precise and exact. The exceptions to the doctrine of complete performance are:
  - Divisible obligations
  - Substantial performance
  - Wrongful prevention
  - Voluntary acceptance of part performance

Note, however, that even under the doctrine of complete performance a supplier may be entitled to keep an advance payment in restitution where there has not been a total failure of consideration. We considered restitution in **Chapter 9**.

Sample questions

Question 1

A landlord wanted to upgrade one of his rental properties. He entered into a contract with a bathroom fitter to remove the old bathroom fittings and to replace them with new sanitary ware. The contract price was £8,000. The landlord paid the builder £500 in advance and agreed to pay the balance on completion. The work was finished but the shower tray leaks (as it was not sealed properly) and so the shower cannot be used. The landlord is refusing to pay the balance of the contract price.

If the builder sued for breach of contract, which of the following would be the most likely legal outcome?

A The builder would be awarded £7,500.

B The builder would keep £500 but not be entitled to any more money.

C The builder would be awarded £7,500 less the cost of properly sealing the shower tray.

D The builder would have to forfeit £500 and not be entitled to any more money.

E The builder would be awarded a reasonable sum in restitution for the work he had done.

Answer

C is correct. There has been substantial performance as the work had been finished but appears to be only slightly defective.

The builder is not entitled to £7,500 as the work was not precise/exact (the doctrine of complete performance) and so A is wrong.

B is wrong. The builder would be entitled to keep £500 in restitution (as there has not been a total failure of consideration) but would be entitled to more money due to having substantially performed the contract.

D is wrong. The builder can keep £500 advance payment in restitution as there was not a total failure of consideration.

E is wrong. The builder is not entitled to a reasonable sum for what he did as there was no voluntary acceptance of part performance (*Sumpter v Hedges*).

Question 2

A client owns a warehouse and agreed to let it on terms including the following:

RENT	£200 per month payable in advance on the first day of each month
TERM	One year from and including 1 March
ROOF	Landlord to repair the roof within first two weeks of the Term

The tenant paid the rent on 1 March and the client carried out the repairs to the roof at a cost of £500. Then on 2 April the warehouse was completely destroyed by an accidental fire and will take at least 10 months to repair. The tenant had not paid the rent due on 1 April.

Which of the following statements describes the most likely legal position?

A The tenant will be liable to pay the rent for the full term as a lease of land cannot be frustrated.

B The lease will come to an end as a matter of law but the tenant will be liable for breach of contract if he does not pay the rent that was due on 1 April.

C If the client sues the tenant for non-payment of rent the tenant may claim the contract is frustrated.

D If the contract is frustrated the tenant must be refunded £200 rent paid in March and the client will be entitled to £500 to cover the cost of repairing the roof.

E If the contract is frustrated neither party will be in breach and they can elect to treat the contract as at an end.

Answer

C is correct. Whether the contract is in fact frustrated would depend on whether there was a valid force majeure clause or the lease otherwise included an express provision on the matter.

A is wrong as a lease of land may be frustrated eg if the event or change of circumstances makes performance totally different.

B is wrong. If a contract is frustrated both parties are released from future obligations as a matter of law and neither party will be liable for breach.

D is wrong. Repayment of expenses incurred is at the discretion of the court and the most the landlord would be entitled to here is £400 (ie the total paid and payable by the tenant at the time of the frustrating event).

E is wrong because if a contract is frustrated the contract automatically comes to an end.

Question 3

A client hired a holiday cottage from a company for the month of August for £2,000. The client paid £200 immediately and agreed to pay the balance of £1,800 on 31 August. The company agreed to put locks on all of the cottage windows. On 8 August the cottage was destroyed by fire. The company had spent £250 on fitting the window locks.

Assuming that the contract is frustrated, which one of the following best describes the client's legal position?

A The company can keep £200 paid in advance and the client will have to pay the £1,800 due on the 31 August or otherwise be in breach of contract.

B   The company can keep the £200 the client paid on the making of the contract and the client will have to pay a further £50 to cover the expenses incurred by the company.

C   The client can get back the £200 she paid on making the contract and would not have to pay anything else to the company.

D   The court may allow the company to retain some or all of the £200 the client paid on making the contract and award a just sum for the use of the cottage.

E   The client will have to pay £500 for the benefit of having used the cottage and contribute a reasonable sum towards the expenses incurred by the company.

Answer

D is correct. Under s 1(2) of the LR(FC)A 1943 (there is nothing in the facts to suggest that this Act does not apply) a court may allow a party who has incurred expenses in performing the contract to recover some or all of these out of the total money paid and payable before the frustrating event. Also under s 1(3) a court should award a 'just sum' for any benefit incurred taking into account any money forfeited under s 1(2) and the effect the frustrating event had on the benefit. The client had enjoyed 7 days' full use of the cottage.

A is wrong because if a contract is frustrated the parties are discharged from future obligations so the client does not have to pay the £1,800.

B and C are wrong. Section 1(2) of the LR(FC)A 1943 provides that a court may allow a party who has incurred expenses in performing the contract to recover some or all of these but only out of money paid and payable before the frustrating event. So here the court may allow the company to retain some or all of the £200 but this is the maximum they can get.

E is wrong. A just sum for the use of the cottage may not be £500 and in relation to the expenses incurred the most the court could award would be £200 but up to that sum the court would have complete discretion.

PART 5
VITIATING FACTORS

11 Misrepresentation

11.1	Introduction	116
11.2	Categories of pre-contract statements	116
11.3	Definition of misrepresentation	118
11.4	Types of misrepresentation and damages	119
11.5	Rescission	121

SQE1 syllabus

This chapter will enable you to achieve the SQE1 assessment specification in relation to functioning legal knowledge concerned with false preliminary statements and in particular misrepresentation.

Note that, for SQE1, candidates are not usually required to recall specific case names or cite statutory or regulatory authorities. Cases are provided for illustrative purposes only.

Learning outcomes

By the end of this chapter you will be able to apply relevant core legal principles and rules appropriately and effectively, at the level of a competent newly qualified solicitor in practice, to realistic client-based and ethical problems and situations in the following areas:

- identifying and classifying actionable false preliminary statements;
- advising on the remedies for misrepresentation; and
- evaluating the different remedies available for breach of contract and misrepresentation.

Contract

11.1 Introduction

One of the most common ways in which the formation of a contract is rendered defective is when one of the parties has misled the other party into entering into the contract. People make misleading statements for numerous reasons, eg from commercial pressure to 'clinch a deal' in a take-over; 'over-stepping the mark' with inflated sales talk to a customer; or even just innocent error. Whichever it is, misleading statements may be actionable in what is known as 'misrepresentation'.

The law on misrepresentation can be considered in the following four stages:

(a) Categories of pre-contract statements

(b) Definition of misrepresentation

(c) Types of misrepresentation

(d) Remedies

So, first of all, we need to categorise the statement made to decide whether it actually formed part of the contract (ie was a term) or whether it was simply an inducement to enter the contract (ie a representation). Then we must identify what counts as a misrepresentation, so we need to define it and apply it to the false preliminary statement that has been made. If a misrepresentation, we then need to determine the type of misrepresentation as this will affect the remedies available to the misrepresentee (ie the party who had been misled).

11.2 Categories of pre-contract statements

Typically preliminary statements fall into the following three categories:

- Sales puff (ie extravagant sales talk that is not meant to be believed and so is not actionable if untrue).

- A contract term (which will give rise to an action for breach if untrue; see **Chapters 8** and **9** for remedies for breach).

- A representation (which may be actionable as a misrepresentation).

For a false preliminary statement to be actionable it must either amount to a term of the contract or otherwise be a misrepresentation.

The law has set out some tests to help us decide between the different categories of preliminary statements. The primary test is the *common intention of the parties* when they entered the contract. If that intention is not clear, there are a number of guidelines that the court will consider, namely:

- Whether one party had greater skill or knowledge of the subject matter.

  If an expert makes a false preliminary statement to a non-expert the statement may well be deemed to be a term of the contract; conversely, if a non-expert makes a false preliminary statement to an expert the statement is more likely to be deemed a simple representation

- Whether a statement made verbally was repeated in a written contract before it was agreed.

  If so the statement is definitely a term but if not, it could well be just a representation.

- Whether the recipient of the statement made clear it was of vital importance.

  If so the statement will almost certainly be a term.

- Whether the statement maker invited the other party to verify it.

    If so the statement may well be just a representation. Whereas if the statement maker had told the other party not to bother checking it, the statement is more likely to be a term.

- Whether there was a lapse of time between the statement being made and the contract being formed.

    The longer the time lapse the more likely the statement will be held to be a representation.

It is not a scoring system. Some of the guidelines tend to carry greater weight than the others. Set out below are some examples to show how the guidelines may operate in practice.

⭐ Examples

Situation	Term	Representation	Reason
1. Natasha wanted to buy vegetables for sale in her health food shop. She told the seller that it was vital that the produce was organic, otherwise she would not be interested in buying it. The seller assured her it was organic and she bought the produce. She has now discovered that chemicals have been used.	√		A statement is likely to be a term if the recipient of the statement makes it clear that the statement is of vital importance.
2. Anoushka wanted to buy a boat. The seller said that it was sound but advised her to have it surveyed. Anoushka did not bother to do so. She bought the boat and has now discovered it is defective.		√	A statement is unlikely to be a term if the maker asks the other party to verify it. This question tends to indicate that the seller did not intend their previous statement to be a term. Conversely, if the seller tells the buyer not to bother with a survey, this points to a statement about the quality of goods being a term.
3. Priti advertises her motorbike for sale in the local paper. Relying on the registration papers, she tells Robin, a private buyer, that the date of manufacture of the bike is 1992. A week later Robin and Priti enter into a written contract that contains no mention of the date of the bike. It turns out to be a much earlier model.		√	This is more likely to be a representation. The written agreement made no mention of the age of the bike and Priti is relying on the registration documents. She does not have any special skill or knowledge. There is also a new factor ie the lapse of time between the making of the statement and the contract. This suggests that it is more likely to be a representation.

If a preliminary statement is deemed to be a term and the term is broken (so it is not what it is promised to be), this will give rise to a claim for breach of contract and the innocent party can pursue remedies for that as appropriate (see **Chapters 8** and **9**). But even if the statement that induced a contract was not a term of the contract it may still be actionable if what was said amounts to a 'misrepresentation'.

11.3 Definition of misrepresentation

A misrepresentation is:

> An untrue statement of fact made by one party to a contract, by words or conduct, to the other contracting party, which induced the other to enter into the contract

We are going to break this down into the four key elements of 'untrue statement', 'fact', 'made by one party to a contract ... to the other contracting party' and 'induced' the contract.

11.3.1 An untrue statement

So the first requirement is that there be an untrue statement. This may be oral, in writing or by conduct. Remember actions can speak as loudly as words.

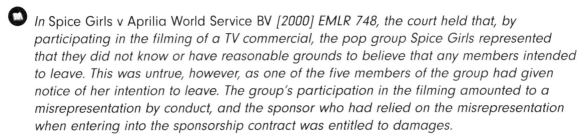

In Spice Girls v Aprilia World Service BV *[2000] EMLR 748, the court held that, by participating in the filming of a TV commercial, the pop group Spice Girls represented that they did not know or have reasonable grounds to believe that any members intended to leave. This was untrue, however, as one of the five members of the group had given notice of her intention to leave. The group's participation in the filming amounted to a misrepresentation by conduct, and the sponsor who had relied on the misrepresentation when entering into the sponsorship contract was entitled to damages.*

Conduct should be distinguished from silence. As a general rule there is no obligation to disclose material facts before you enter into a contract. So, for instance, a seller of property does not have to disclose an inherent problem with it. You may have heard of the 'Buyer beware' principle – well, this is an example of it.

However, silence may amount to misrepresentation:

(a) where there is a fiduciary relationship between the parties (eg solicitor and client or trustee and beneficiary);

(b) where the contract is one of the utmost good faith (eg an insurance contract);

(c) where there has been a half-truth (ie where what was not said positively distorts what was actually said, eg if a car is advertised 'one lady owner' and this is true but it ignores the other previous owners who happened to be men, giving the misleading impression that there has been just one owner and that the one owner was a lady – the moral is to tell the whole truth, or nothing at all); and

(d) where a statement of fact is true when made but a change of circumstances occurs before the contract is formed that makes the statement untrue, and the change is not disclosed.

11.3.2 A statement of fact, not opinion or future intention

Not all statements, even if they turn out to be untrue, count as 'misrepresentations'. The law requires that the statement be one of fact, as opposed to a statement of future intention or a statement being a reasonably held opinion of a party. Note, however, that if a party lies about their intention or otherwise states an opinion for which there are no facts on which it can reasonably be based, then these will be statements of fact. In the first case the maker of the statement is mispresenting the state of their mind (which is a fact) and in the second case the statement maker is misrepresenting that they *are* in possession of facts on which their opinion can reasonably be formulated.

Example

You are thinking of buying a large house that has a tenant living in part of it. The seller tells you the tenant is a 'most desirable' tenant. You buy the property and then discover that the tenant has been in arrears with rent for some time and the seller knew this.

This statement would be a statement of fact and not opinion since the maker of the statement was aware that the tenant was in arrears with the rent and therefore would not be regarded as desirable.

11.3.3 Statement must be made by one contracting party to the other

If the maker of the statement is not the other contracting party, there cannot be a claim for misrepresentation although it may be possible to bring a claim in tort for negligent misstatement or deceit.

11.3.4 The statement must induce the other party into entering into the contract

The fact that the statement must induce the representee (ie the party to whom the statement was made) to enter into the contract is often described in terms that the representee must rely on the statement. There are various circumstances in which the representor may make a statement but, nevertheless, the law does not regard it as one on which the representee relied in entering into the contract, eg because the representee had appointed an expert to verify the representation and had relied solely on the expert's report.

Note however, that the statement need not be the only inducement to enter the contract. It is enough that it was at least *a* reason for doing so.

11.4 Types of misrepresentation and damages

Just as we have to classify contract terms to determine the remedies available for breach, the same is true with misrepresentations. The remedies for misrepresentation (in particular, damages) differ according to the degree of culpability with which they are made.

At the one end of the scale are deliberate lies. In the middle, statements made 'carelessly' but not known to be false. Finally there are statements made honestly and carefully, but which just happen to be untrue.

11.4.1 Fraudulent misrepresentation

Misrepresentation is only fraudulent if made:

- with knowledge that it is false; or
- without belief in its truth; or
- recklessly, not caring whether it is true or false.

Nothing short of some proof of fraud will suffice and this may be very difficult to establish.

Damages in the tort of deceit have always been available for fraudulent misrepresentation. The measure of these damages is how much the misrepresentee is 'out-of-pocket' as a result of the misrepresentation, and damages extend to *all* consequential losses. Remoteness of loss does not come into it.

 The case of East v Maurer *[1991] 2 All ER 733 involved a fraudulent misrepresentation by the seller of a hair dressing salon. East had bought the business in reliance on the seller's deliberate false assertion that he (Maurer) intended to stop working at his other hair dressing salon in the same town. As a result of the unexpected competition from Maurer, East's business was unsuccessful and was eventually sold at a loss. One of the questions*

the Court of Appeal had to consider was what could be claimed in damages to represent the loss of profit suffered by East as a result of the false statement. The court concluded that tortious principles should be used to calculate the loss of profit suffered – meaning that the innocent party should be put into the position he would have been in, had the misrepresentation not been made. If the misrepresentation had not been made East would not have bought that particular hair dressing salon; he would have bought a similar one instead. So East was awarded damages representing the difference between the profit he in fact made and the profit he would have made had he bought a similar business. This is a different calculation to that which is used when determining damages under ordinary breach of contract principles. There, the aim of damages is to put the innocent party, so far as money can do it, into the position they would have been in, had the contract been properly performed ie loss of bargain damages. So if damages in East v Maurer had been awarded on this basis East would have got a sum representing the difference between the profit he actually made and the profit he would have made had the statement been true.

11.4.2 Negligent misrepresentation

Negligent misrepresentation concerns statements that were made carelessly. These statements are governed by s 2(1) of the Misrepresentation Act (MA) 1967. This section provides for the misrepresentor to be liable to pay damages where, although the belief in the truth of the statement was honestly held, it was not held on reasonable grounds. The section reverses the normal burden of proof of who has to prove the belief was held reasonably; it requires the misrepresentor to prove they made the statement on reasonable grounds. So the claimant only has to establish the misrepresentation and loss; it is then up to the defendant to prove it was 'honest and reasonable' if they wish to avoid paying damages under the section. This can be very difficult to do.

 The difficulty faced by the party making the misrepresentation in discharging the burden of proof under s 2(1) is illustrated by Howard Marine & Dredging v Ogden *[1978] 2 All ER 1134 (CA). In this case, a representative of the owner of a barge (the defendant) told a potential charterer that its capacity was about 1,600 tonnes. He based this figure on his recollection of the relevant entry in the* Lloyd's Register, *which stated that the capacity was 1,800 tonnes. The capacity was in fact much less, and the representative would have discovered this if he had consulted the ship's documents. The charterers later sought to claim damages from the defendant under s 2(1) of the MA 1967 and succeeded.*

The defendant failed to prove that its representative had had reasonable grounds to believe in the truth of the statement. The representative had only consulted Lloyd's Register. *He could have looked at the ship's documents, which stated the correct capacity of the barge.*

Furthermore, even though these statements may only have been made carelessly (as opposed to fraudulently) damages are nevertheless assessed in the same way as for fraudulent misrepresentation. So all consequential losses are recoverable and the aim is to put the innocent party in the position they would have been in if the misrepresentation had not been made.

This begs the question why a misrepresentee would bother trying to prove fraud. Under s 2(1) of the MA 1967 the misrepresentor will be liable in damages to the same extent as if they had been fraudulent, unless they can effectively disprove negligence. As we have seen this is a difficult burden of proof to discharge.

11.4.3 Innocent misrepresentation

If the misrepresentor can establish that they had reasonable grounds to believe their statement was true, then this would still be a misrepresentation, but one that falls into the innocent misrepresentation category. It is not negligent so it is not covered by section 2(1) of the Act. As such, no damages are available as of right for an innocent misrepresentation.

However, note that, whilst damages may not available, the misrepresentee may still be able to rescind the contract, if rescission is not barred – see below.

11.5 Rescission

We have seen that damages for misrepresentation depend on the type of misrepresentation but the effect of *any* misrepresentation is to make the contract voidable. In other words, the misrepresentee has a choice – they may either affirm the contract (decide to keep going with it) or rescind the contract (decide to get out of it). Misrepresentation does not make a contract void per se.

So if a party has been misled into a contract and does not want to affirm it, one option is to get out of the contract. This is rescission. It is also known as 'setting aside' a contract. It is a remedy that, in principle, is available for all types of misrepresentation and may be awarded in addition to damages.

Rescission involves the mutual restoration of all benefits received, in order to place both of the parties, as far as money can do it, back in their pre-contractual positions. Think of it as hitting the rewind button – to go back to the start.

⭐ Example

Zena has bought a car from Keith. Keith has delivered the car to her and she has paid him £7,000. She still has a further £500 to pay and she will pay this when he installs a Sat Nav in the car.

Assume that Keith has made a misrepresentation to Zena, eg about the age or mileage of the car. If Zena rescinds:

- *Zena will return the car to Keith.*
- *Keith will return the £7,000 Zena has already paid.*
- *Keith will not have to install a Sat Nav.*
- *Zena will not have to pay Keith the further £500.*

Rescission is an equitable remedy. As such it is awarded at the discretion of the court and the right to rescind will be lost in certain situations. When this happens, there is said to be a bar to rescission There are four bars to rescission:

(a) Affirmation. The innocent party on discovering the misrepresentation may elect to treat the contract as continuing – and doing nothing may amount to affirmation. Once the innocent party has affirmed the contract they cannot then change their mind and rescind.

(b) Undue delay.

(c) Where an innocent purchaser has acquired an interest in the subject matter of the contract before purported rescission of the contract.

(d) Where it is impossible substantially to restore goods or property.

Undue delay, like affirmation, is an equitable bar to rescission and is illustrated by the case of *Leaf v International Galleries* [1950] 2 KB 86.

 In Leaf v International Galleries *the claimant had bought a painting that had been described to him as an original John Constable. Five years later, he discovered it had not*

been painted by Constable. As a result, the claimant sought to rescind the contract under which he had bought the painting, but his action failed due to lapse of time.

The claimant had had the chance to examine the picture within a few days of purchase and discover the misrepresentation. A delay of five years meant he could not rescind the contract.

The *Leaf* case illustrates that, in calculating delay, the court does not necessarily look at when the misrepresentation was actually discovered but at when it should have been discovered.

However, the principle that time runs from when the misrepresentation should have been discovered does not apply to a fraudulent misrepresentation. If there is a fraudulent misrepresentation then time runs from when the misrepresentation was actually discovered.

The other equitable bar to rescission is where an innocent purchaser acquires an interest in the property before the contract is rescinded.

 In Car & Universal Finance v Caldwell [1964] 1 All ER 290 a rogue bought a car as a result of misrepresentation and then disappeared. As soon as the innocent party (the seller) discovered that he had been tricked he notified the police and the Automobile Association (AA), and that had the effect of immediately transferring ownership of the car back to him. This was important on the facts, as following notification to the police and AA the rogue had sold the car to an innocent third party, and the main question before the court was which of the two innocent parties (ie the original seller or innocent buyer) should get the car, and which should be left having to sue the rogue for his loss. As the original seller was deemed to have rescinded the contract (and thus regained ownership of the car) before the sale to the innocent purchaser, the court found in favour of the original seller.

Had the facts been different and the rogue had resold the car to the innocent purchaser before the police and AA had been notified, rescission would have been barred. An innocent purchaser who acquires an interest in the property before the contract is avoided is one of the bars to rescission.

The final bar to rescission is a practical bar ie where it is impossible for a party substantially to restore goods or property to the other.

 A case in which this bar operated is Crystal Palace FC (2000) Ltd v Iain Dowie [2007] EWHC 1392 (QB). *The claimant had entered into a compromise agreement with the defendant (its former manager) releasing him from his employment contract with the club. Under his employment contract, the defendant had been required to pay the club £1 million compensation if he left prematurely to work for a premiership club. The compromise agreement released the defendant from this obligation to pay the compensation. Very shortly after entering the compromise agreement, the defendant was appointed manager of a premiership club.*

The court held that the defendant had deceived the claimant into entering the compromise agreement, but the court refused an order for rescission. If the compromise agreement had been rescinded, it would have revived the defendant's employment contract with the claimant. The claimant had in the meantime appointed another manager, and the defendant was now employed as a manager of another club. The defendant could not perform two employment contracts at the same time. Practical justice meant the making of appropriate orders for damages but not an order for rescission.

It is for this reason that a contract for the sale of a business is rarely rescinded. A business is likely to have changed its position (eg by entering into contracts with third parties) rendering rescission impossible.

Figure 11.1 summarises the different possible outcomes of misrepresentation.

Figure 11.1 Effect of misrepresentation

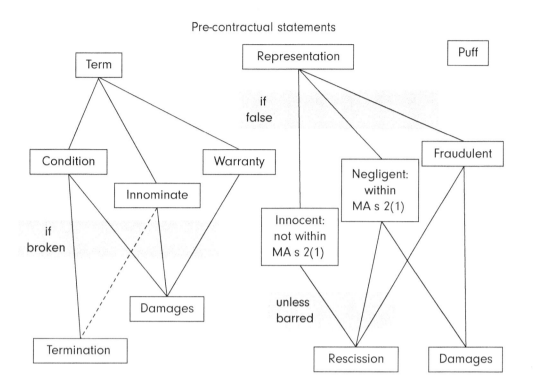

Summary

- For a false preliminary statement to be actionable it must either amount to breach of a contract term or be a misrepresentation.
- The test for deciding whether a preliminary statement is a term or representation is the intention of the parties. To determine this the courts use the following guidelines:
  - Relative skill and knowledge of the parties.
  - Whether the maker of the statement suggested the other party check the accuracy.
  - Timing of the statement.
  - If there is a written contract was any earlier statement included in it?
  - Did the innocent party stress the importance of the statement?
- The definition of misrepresentation is technical. There must be an untrue statement of fact made by one contracting party to the other that acted as an inducement to enter the contract.
- The effect of misrepresentation is to make the contract voidable. The aim of rescission is restitution but rescission may be barred eg by undue delay.
- Damages are available for fraudulent misrepresentation in the tort of deceit and for negligent misrepresentation under s 2(1) of the MA 1967. All consequential losses are recoverable and the aim of damages is to put the innocent party in the financial position it would have been in if the misrepresentation had not been made.

Sample questions

Question 1

A client bought a business for £180,000 having been deliberately misled by the seller as to the gross profit made by the business. After running the business for a few months the client discovered the fraudulent misrepresentation. The client was advised to continue running the business (albeit at a loss) and to try to sell it. The sale of the business went through last week. It sold for £80,000.

If the client sues for misrepresentation, which of the following best explains how damages would be assessed?

A   On an expectation loss basis.

B   On a reliance loss basis for wasted expenditure that was not too remote.

C   On a tortious basis for all consequential losses.

D   On a tortious basis and so would not extend to any loss of profit.

E   For any loss that was not too remote the client would get damages to put him in the same position as if the misrepresentation had not been made.

Answer

C is correct. Damages under s 2(1) are awarded on the same basis as if the misrepresentation had been made fraudulently and so extend to all consequential losses and the measure is as if the misrepresentation had never been made.

A and B are wrong as they are ways of assessing damages for breach of contract.

D is wrong as damages for loss of profit may be assessed on a tortious basis (*East v Maurer*).

E is wrong as all consequential losses are recoverable – remoteness is not an issue.

Question 2

In May a buyer entered into a contract to buy a beauty salon having been deliberately misled by the seller as to the gross profit made by the salon over the previous three years. The buyer made extensive alterations to the salon including the addition of a new treatment room. Then in August the buyer discovered the fraudulent misrepresentation and decided he no longer wanted the salon.

Could the buyer rescind the contract of sale?

A   No, because rescission would be barred by undue delay.

B   No, because rescission is an equitable remedy and damages would adequately compensate the buyer.

C   No, because restitution is impossible.

D   Yes, because rescission is potentially available for all forms of misrepresentation and the buyer has not affirmed the contract.

E   Yes, because rescission is always available for fraudulent misrepresentation.

Answer

C is correct. As the buyer made extensive alterations to the salon including the addition of a new treatment room restitution would be impossible.

A is wrong as rescission would not be barred by delay. With fraudulent misrepresentation time runs from discovering the misrepresentation.

B is wrong as rescission may be awarded in addition to damages.

D is wrong. Rescission is potentially available for all forms of misrepresentation but would be barred on the facts as restitution is impossible.

E is wrong as rescission is not available as of right for any misrepresentation.

Question 3

A client saw a vase in an antique shop. The client thought it was very rare and worth far more than the price asked. The owner of the shop overheard the client telling someone this on the phone. The owner knew the vase was not rare and valuable but did not tell the client. The client bought the vase and has now discovered the vase is worth less than the price paid.

Does the client have a cause of action against the owner of the shop?

A   Yes, because the owner of the shop made a misrepresentation: the owner should have corrected the mistake.

B   Yes, because the owner of the shop would be in breach of an implied term that the sale price was a reasonable price for the vase.

C   Yes, because the owner of the shop made a fraudulent misrepresentation by positively deceiving the client.

D   No, because the general rule is 'buyer beware'.

E   No, because the client acted unconscionably in trying to buy the vase for less than it was worth.

Answer

D is correct The general rule is 'buyer beware'

A is wrong. The owner of the shop had not made a misrepresentation. Generally there is no obligation to say anything unless specifically asked.

B is wrong. The price was agreed. Consideration need not be adequate – see **Chapter 3.1.1.**

C is wrong as there was no positive deception; indeed there was no misrepresentation at all.

E is wrong. There is nothing wrong in trying to secure a good bargain.

12 Duress and Undue Influence

12.1	Introduction	128
12.2	Duress	128
12.3	Undue influence	131

SQE1 syllabus

This chapter will enable you to achieve the SQE1 assessment specification in relation to functioning legal knowledge concerned with duress and undue influence.

Note that, for SQE1, candidates are not usually required to recall specific case names or cite statutory or regulatory authorities. Cases are provided for illustrative purposes only.

Learning outcomes

By the end of this chapter you will be able to apply relevant core legal principles and rules appropriately and effectively, at the level of a competent newly qualified solicitor in practice, to realistic client-based and ethical problems and situations in the following areas:

- advising on the validity of contracts and contractual variations entered into under illegitimate threats and pressure;
- establishing duress and undue influence; and
- advising on how the undue influence of a third party debtor may vitiate a security contract.

12.1 Introduction

The essence of agreement, upon which contract law is based, is that the parties freely consent to the agreed terms. We saw in the last chapter how a party who has been misled into a contract may potentially get the contract set aside. The same holds true where a party has been illegitimately coerced or pressured by the other party into an agreement. So if there has been duress or undue influence exerted upon an innocent party the resulting contract, or variation to a contract, is voidable, ie capable of being set aside (**Figure 12.1**). But, whereas with misrepresentation the innocent party may sometimes be entitled to damages, the only remedy for duress and undue influence is rescission.

Figure 12.1 Vitiating factors

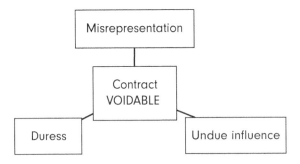

12.2 Duress

Duress may take the form of violence or illegitimate threats or pressure that coerce a party into entering a contract or varying a contract, and the burden of proving duress is on the party who alleges it.

Cases that involve threats of physical violence are quite rare. But if there is a threat of violence, sometimes referred to as duress to the person, made at the time a contract is being made, then it can amount to duress *if* it can be proved that the threats were at least *a* reason for entering the contract. So duress need *not* be the *only* reason why the innocent party entered the contract, but it must have induced the contract in some way.

In the modern commercial world, threats to a person's economic or business interests are far more common.

The first thing to remember is that legitimate commercial pressure will not affect the contract. A threat to take business elsewhere, sell to a competitor or not to give a discount in future are all likely to be regarded as legitimate commercial pressure. To amount to economic duress, the threat must be an *improper* or *illegitimate* threat (like a threat to breach a contract or to commit a tort). It can sometimes be difficult to draw a distinction between legitimate commercial pressure and illegitimate threats that may amount to economic duress.

> *The case of* Carillion Construction Ltd v Felix (UK) Ltd *[2001] BLR 1 set out what must be proved in order to establish that economic duress had been present. There must be pressure:*
>
> *(a) whose practical effect is that there is compulsion on, or a lack of practical choice for, the victim;*

(b) which is illegitimate; and

(c) which is a significant *cause inducing the claimant to enter into the contract.*

In determining whether there has been illegitimate pressure, the court will take into account a range of factors, including whether:

- there has been an actual or a threatened breach of contract;
- the threat was made in good or bad faith; or
- the victim protested at the time.

These have become a list of guidelines to use when deciding if illegitimate pressure is involved. Remember, though, that illegitimate pressure must be distinguished from the rough and tumble of the pressures of normal commercial bargaining.

⭐ Example

Krista owns a restaurant. For the past 10 years, Peter, who owns Hill Farm, has supplied her with organic fruit, vegetables and other products. Their contract is renegotiated every six months. In the last negotiations Peter told Krista that unless she agreed to pay 80% more for the products Peter would no longer be her supplier. There was no other local farm that could supply Krista with organic products and so she agreed.

This is tough on Krista, but appears to amount to no more than the normal commercial pressures of business. The balance of supply and demand is often the determining factor behind hard bargains, not duress. Whilst Krista has no practical choice as to whether or not to accept, there is no illegitimate pressure here that would force her to agree to the new prices.

12.2.1 Effect of duress

Duress makes an original, or renegotiated, contract *voidable*. It is a similar outcome to that which follows a proven misrepresentation (**Chapter 11**).

A voidable contract is a valid, binding contract unless, and until, it is rescinded by the innocent party. On the face of it, the innocent party can either rescind or affirm the contract (ie treat it as ongoing), but once they affirm the contract, the innocent party cannot then change their mind.

So the remedy for duress, should the victim choose to use it, is rescission. The innocent party must notify the other party that it wants to rescind. In addition, the innocent party can apply to the court for an order of rescission. The innocent party may have to do this, if the other refuses to return money or property.

When a contract is rescinded, neither party need perform any future obligations and each party should return money or property transferred under the contract.

Remember, though, that rescission may be barred. The main bars to rescission are:

(a) Affirmation

(b) Undue delay

(c) A bona fide purchaser

(d) Impossible to restore goods or property

 The case of North Ocean Shipping v Hyundai Construction (The Atlantic Baron) *[1979] QB 705 involved the construction of a ship called 'The Atlantic Baron'. Building started, but the shipbuilders demanded more money and threatened to stop work unless the claimants*

agreed to pay the extra money. The claimants agreed to pay the extra money as they had no practical choice but to agree to the demand. They desperately needed the ship to be finished on time as they had made a contract to hire out the ship on completion. The ship was delivered on time and the shipbuilders were then paid.

Eight months later the claimants asked for repayment of the extra money on the grounds of duress. Here, the court held that there was economic duress but they refused to rescind the variation for two reasons – affirmation and delay. The court found that when the claimants paid the extra money, they were no longer under any sort of threat or pressure. There was apparently no danger at that time that the shipbuilders would refuse to deliver. Therefore the action of the claimants in paying appeared to be an affirmation of the variation. Also, the bar of delay applied, as the claimants left it eight months before asking for the return of their money.

Perhaps a better course of action for the ship owners might have been not *to pay the extra money when it became due. They would then have been able to use duress as a* defence *to any action for the extra money owed.*

 This is illustrated by Atlas Express v Kafco *[1989] 1 All ER 641.*

The claimants were a road haulage company. The defendants were a small firm of manufacturers. The defendants had managed to secure a contract with Woolworths stores around the country. The defendants entered into a contract with the claimants whereby the claimants agreed to transport the defendants' goods to the various Woolworths stores. The goods were to be transported in cartons and the defendants agreed to pay £1.10 per carton. The contract did not specify how many cartons the defendants would supply per load.

For the first load the defendants supplied 200 cartons. The claimants had expected more. They thought there would be 400–600 cartons. The claimants refused to make any more deliveries unless the defendants agreed to pay a minimum of £400 per load. The defendants were a small business. It would have been difficult for them to find another haulage company to deliver to Woolworths on time. If the goods were not delivered on time, their business relationship with Woolworths would have been ruined. They therefore agreed to pay the extra amount, but in the event did not do so and that is why they were sued. Kafco raised economic duress as a defence and succeeded.

12.2.2 Link between economic duress and consideration

In the above case (which was decided just before *Williams v Roffey* that we looked at in **Chapter 3** in the context of promises to pay more for the same) Kafco also argued that Atlas had given no consideration for its promise to pay extra money on the basis that Atlas was simply performing an existing contractual duty. The argument succeeded.

With upward variations, the general principle is indeed that performance of an existing contractual duty owed to the other party is not consideration for a promise of extra money. So if a party who promised to pay more was effectively forced into the agreement, they could simply argue that there had been no consideration given for that promise.

But the courts now take a more practical approach to variations of commercial contracts, and performing an existing contractual obligation *can* be good consideration for a promise of more money, provided the person promising the money obtains a *practical benefit* in return (*Williams v Roffey*). If, however, notwithstanding a practical benefit, the promise to pay more was only made under duress then the variation (promise to pay more) will be voidable and capable of being set aside.

In cases such as this it is important to remember that it is only the later variation that is affected by the duress, and therefore only the variation that will be rescinded, not the original contract.

⭐ Example

Kelvin Ltd agrees to deliver machinery to Dan Harvey Tools for £3,000. Dan is a sole trader. Two days before the delivery date, Kelvin tells Dan that it will not deliver unless Dan pays an additional £500. Dan protests but pays the money as he feels he has no other choice. Kelvin delivers the machinery on time. Dan now wants rescission.

Let us assume that all the ingredients for duress are satisfied and none of the bars to rescission apply. It is only the variation that will be rescinded. Kelvin will have to repay the extra £500. Kelvin will not have to repay the original £3,000 and Dan will not have to return the machinery as these were terms agreed in the main contract and were not subject to the duress.

12.3 Undue influence

In many ways, the doctrine of undue influence is very similar to duress. Undue influence, like duress, makes a contract voidable. So the remedy available, if undue influence is found, is rescission and the same bars to rescission apply as for duress. Also like duress there is no remedy of damages. But as we will see shortly there are some significant differences eg in terms of what needs to be established.

There is no precise definition of undue influence. Basically it is:

- influence that goes beyond what is regarded as acceptable; or
- where one party is in a position to influence another and takes unfair advantage of that position.

Undue influence consists not of threats or violence but of influence that goes beyond what is regarded as acceptable. Just as it can be difficult to decide where legitimate commercial pressure ends and economic duress begins, it can be difficult to say at what point acceptable influence becomes 'undue' influence. The approach adopted by the law is to identify relationships that are unequal and then to consider whether the transaction resulted from the dominant person abusing that relationship.

12.3.1 Actual and presumed undue influence

Thinking back to duress, you may recall that the onus is on the innocent party to prove duress. That is not necessarily the case with undue influence, because as well as actual undue influence, which has been proved on the facts, there is *presumed* undue influence. Basically, undue influence will be presumed where there is a fiduciary relationship – or a relationship of trust and confidence – between the parties *and* a transaction occurs that calls for explanation (**Figure 12.2**). As undue influence tends to be something that goes on 'behind closed doors', it will often be very difficult to prove, so most innocent parties will try to raise a presumption of undue influence.

12.3.1.1 Actual undue influence

⭕ *There are few reported cases in which actual undue influence has been established but one case in which the evidence of the innocent party (supported by a witness) was preferred is* Daniel v Drew [2005] EWCA Civ 507. *Mrs Drew was an elderly lady who intensely disliked confrontation and was afraid of her nephew and the prospect of going to court. So when he told her to sign the contract under the threat of taking court action, she had felt unable to refuse.*

Note that, unlike duress, the threat *may* be entirely legal, such as, in this case, taking court action.

Figure 12.2 Types of undue influence

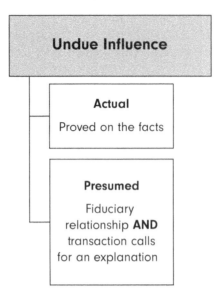

12.3.1.2 Presumed undue influence

For undue influence to be presumed, there must be:

- a relationship of trust and confidence; *and*
- a transaction that calls for an explanation.

Relationship of trust and confidence

In certain categories of relationship (eg solicitor and client, doctor and patient), it is irrebuttably presumed that one party places trust and confidence in the other. This is also the case with parents and children (under 18), and religious advisers and followers. Note it is not, however, presumed in a relationship of husband and wife.

In any case where the relationship is *not* presumed to be one of trust and confidence, such as husband and wife, the innocent party will have to prove this. For example, a wife may be able to prove that she did in fact place trust and confidence in her husband in relation to financial matters.

 A case in which a relationship of trust and confidence was established on the facts is O'Sullivan v Management Agency Ltd [1985] QB 428. Here the relationship of trust and confidence was between Gilbert O'Sullivan, a young, unknown singer/songwriter, and his manager. Mr O'Sullivan succeeded in having a number of management, agency, recording and publishing agreements and transfers of copyright set aside for undue influence. In fact, undue influence has been a common argument in the music industry when new talent entering into agreements have later regretted their agreements once they have had commercial success. Fortunately, processes have now become established to protect both the artists and their management from such disputes.

The transaction must call for an explanation

To raise any presumption of undue influence, though, it is not enough for there simply to be a relationship of trust and confidence between the parties. In addition, the transaction that the parties enter into must be such that it is not easy to explain just by the relationship between them; in other words, the transaction must call for explanation eg where a party enters a contract that is not for their benefit or that exposes them to risk.

Lastly, note that, as with most presumptions, the presumption of undue influence is rebuttable. For example, it could be rebutted if there was evidence to show that the innocent party had taken independent advice.

Figure 12.3 sets out the steps for establishing undue influence.

Figure 12.3 Is there undue influence?

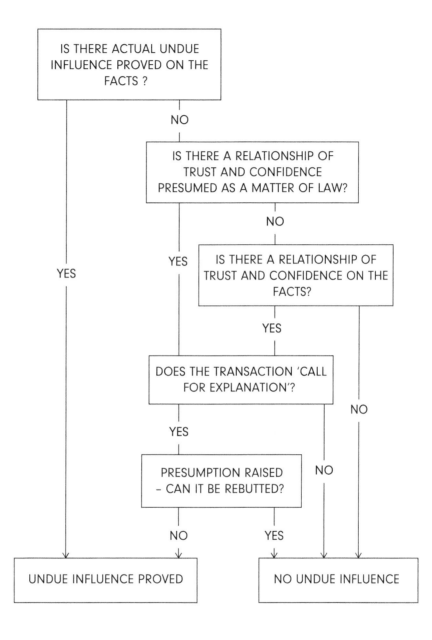

12.3.2 Undue influence and the position of third parties

The law on undue influence has become important over recent years in relation to the notion of tainting a contracting party – typically a commercial lender – with the undue influence of a third party. Let's take a look at the typical situation and consider the legal, practical and commercial issues it raises.

⭐ Example

```
Husband————Undue————>Wife
(Debtor)      influence       (Surety)

Bank<————Loan————>Husband
(Creditor)    agreement

Bank<————Security (guarantee)————>Wife
            agreement
```

A husband's business needs an injection of capital, and he approaches a commercial lender for a loan. The lender is prepared to advance the money, subject to taking security by way of a charge over the matrimonial home. As the matrimonial home is owned jointly by husband and wife, the wife will need to be a party to the security agreement. She would be a surety (ie a person who gives security for the debts of another). As a result of her husband's undue influence, the wife signs the relevant documentation and the husband gets the money he needs for his business.

The husband's business has problems: the loan is not repaid and the lender seeks to enforce its security and repossess the matrimonial home. It is at this stage that the wife alleges undue influence by the husband and asks for the security agreement to be set aside (or rescinded) as a result. If the security agreement is set aside, the lender will have lost its security and will be left suing the husband as an unsecured creditor. If the security agreement is not set aside, the lender will repossess the matrimonial home and the wife will effectively be left without a roof over her head.

The dilemma in this type of situation is that there are two innocent parties, the wife and the lender. To what extent, if any, should either or both of them be offered protection by the law? It would clearly be unfair to a lender if it was always affected by the undue influence of the husband. Also, as a matter of commercial reality, small businesses need loans, and lenders will often insist they are secured, and the main asset that can be offered as security is the matrimonial home.

So, lenders need to be able to take security with some reassurance that they will be able to enforce it if necessary. On the other hand, what about the wife? She trusted her husband and only signed the documentation because he told her to do so. She was not aware of the risks and practical implications involved in what she was doing.

The compromise reached by the courts hinges on whether the creditor had actual or constructive notice of the debtor's (husband's) undue influence. If the creditor had actual or constructive notice of the debtor's impropriety, it will be tainted with it and any security contract obtained as a result will be voidable and capable of being set aside.

● *The leading authority in this area is the House of Lords decision in* Royal Bank of Scotland v Etridge (No 2) [2001] 4 All ER 449. *The wife successfully argued that the bank had constructive notice of her husband's undue influence and so should not get possession of the house.*

The House of Lords stated that a creditor will *have constructive notice if:*

- *it ought to have been* put 'on inquiry'; and
- *it did not take reasonable steps to ensure that the surety was aware of the implications of what they were signing.*

Put on inquiry

A creditor will be put on inquiry in all cases where the relationship between the debtor and surety is non-commercial and the loan is not for their joint benefit. So for example if the husband wrongly states in his loan application that he intends to use the money to buy a holiday home for him and his wife (rather than to play on the stock market, which is his true intention) the creditor will not be put on inquiry. From the loan application there is nothing to alert it to the risk of any wrongdoing on the part of the husband.

Reasonable steps

Once a creditor is put on inquiry, what then are the reasonable steps it should take to make sure the surety is made aware in a meaningful way of the legal implications of what they are signing?

The creditor could have a private meeting with the surety to explain the risks and advise the surety to take independent advice. A 'private meeting' because the surety needs to be removed from the influence of the debtor and if the creditor writes to the surety the correspondence might be intercepted by the debtor.

There are clearly risks involved with this first option and what creditors tend to do is insist the surety takes independent advice from a solicitor. The creditor may well pay for the advice in the knowledge that once it has a certificate from the solicitor saying that the surety has been properly advised then the security it has taken will be upheld. If the surety contends that they were not fully informed of the risks any cause of action will lie against the solicitor and will not in any way impact the validity of the security.

 Although most of the cases have involved a husband taking advantage of his wife, the principles apply equally to other relationships. One case that did not involve a husband and wife is Credit Lyonnais Bank Nederland v Burch *[1997] 1 All ER 144. The case involved an employer (who owned the business) and a junior employee. The employee re-mortgaged her flat to secure the unlimited liabilities of the employer's business in which she had no financial interest. The court decided that there was a presumption of undue influence and the bank was stopped from enforcing the security. Even though several attempts to invite the employee to take independent legal advice were made, she did not do so. On the particular facts the creditor should have insisted the surety took independent legal advice or otherwise not have taken the proposed security.*

Where a creditor is stopped from enforcing its security it will still have an action against the debtor for the sum of money it is owed. It is just that this may be difficult to enforce bearing in mind the financial situation of the debtor.

The position of lenders in relation to undue influence exerted by debtors is summarised in **Figure 12.4**.

Figure 12.4 The effect of undue influence on the lender

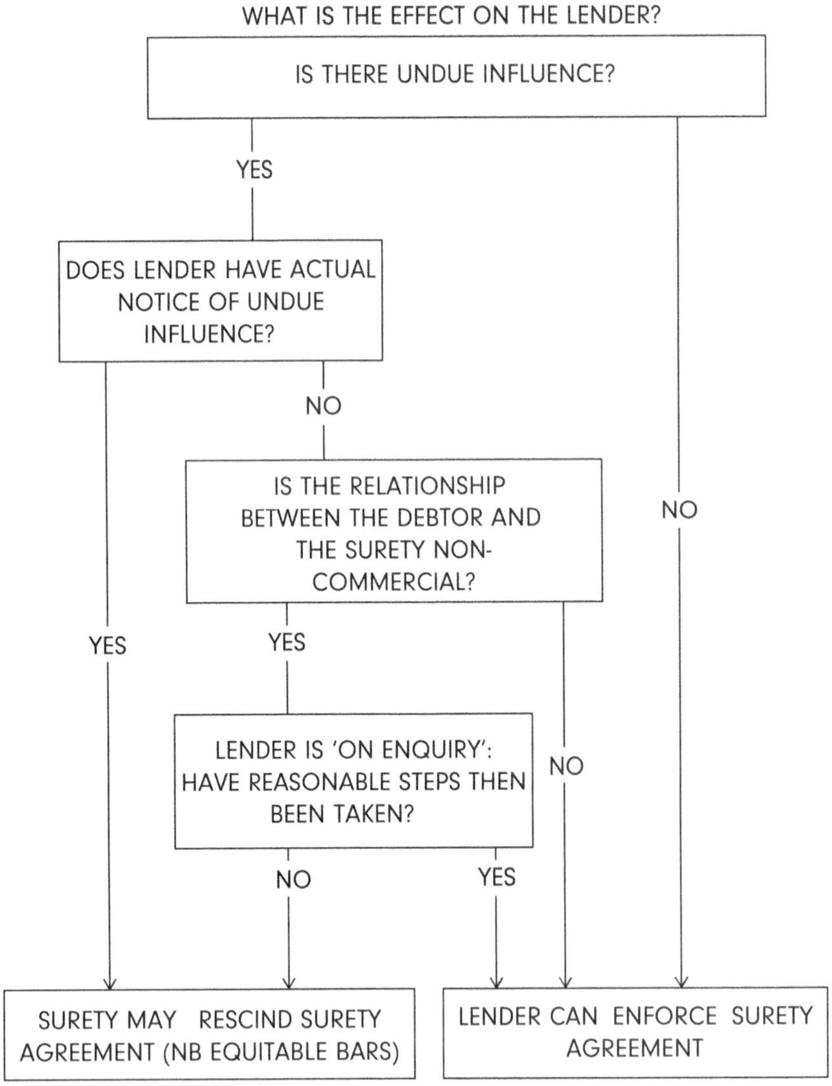

```
                        WHAT IS THE EFFECT ON THE LENDER?
                        ┌─────────────────────────────────┐
                        │    IS THERE UNDUE INFLUENCE?    │
                        └─────────────────────────────────┘
                                      │
                                     YES
                                      │
                ┌─────────────────────┴──────┐
                │ DOES LENDER HAVE ACTUAL    │
                │   NOTICE OF UNDUE          │
                │      INFLUENCE?            │
                └────────────────────────────┘
                     │              │
                     │              NO
                     │              │
                     │      ┌───────┴──────────────┐
                     │      │ IS THE RELATIONSHIP  │
                     │      │ BETWEEN THE DEBTOR   │          NO
                     │      │  AND THE SURETY NON- │
                     │      │     COMMERCIAL?      │
                     │      └──────────────────────┘
                     │              │
                     YES           YES
                     │              │
                     │      ┌───────┴──────────────┐
                     │      │ LENDER IS 'ON ENQUIRY':│ NO
                     │      │ HAVE REASONABLE STEPS  │
                     │      │    THEN BEEN TAKEN?    │
                     │      └────────────────────────┘
                     │              │         │
                     │              NO       YES
                     │              │         │
        ┌────────────┴──────────────┴──┐   ┌──┴──────────────────┐
        │ SURETY MAY RESCIND SURETY    │   │ LENDER CAN ENFORCE  │
        │ AGREEMENT (NB EQUITABLE BARS)│   │   SURETY AGREEMENT  │
        └──────────────────────────────┘   └─────────────────────┘
```

Summary

- The effect of both duress and undue influence is to make contracts voidable. The only remedy is rescission.
- Economic duress arises where there is an illegitimate threat that leaves the other party with no practical choice and that was a factor inducing them to enter the contract or variation.
- Economic duress is particularly relevant in relation to upward variations. Performance of an existing contractual duty owed to the other party will be consideration for a promise to pay more if it confers a practical benefit, but the variation will be voidable if the promise to pay more was made under duress.
- Undue influence arises where a person in a position of trust abuses that position and takes unfair advantage of the other party.

- Undue influence may be established on the facts (actual undue influence) or presumed where there is a position of trust and confidence *and* the transaction calls for an explanation.
- A creditor may be tainted with the undue influence of a third party debtor if it had actual or constructive notice of it.
- A creditor will be put on inquiry in all cases where the relationship between the debtor and surety is non-commercial and the loan is not for their joint benefit.

Sample questions

Question 1

A client manufactures precision parts for the motor industry. Six months ago it won a lucrative contract with a major car manufacturer. To fulfil this contract the client reached agreement with a tool making company ('the Company') to supply certain equipment by the end of last week. Two months ago the Company told the client that it had underestimated costs and would have to charge an extra £6,000 if it was to carry on. The client protested but reluctantly agreed as it could not find another manufacturer to do the job. The equipment was made on time and the client paid the Company £16,000 (ie the original contract price plus the extra £6,000) on delivery.

Which of the following statements best describes the legal position?

A   The client's promise to pay more would not be binding as the Company had given no consideration for it.

B   The contract with the Company could be set aside and the client would be refunded £16,000 because the promise to pay extra was made under duress.

C   The contractual variation would be binding because the Company had conferred a practical benefit and exerted no duress, just hard commercial bargaining.

D   The Company had provided consideration for the extra £6,000 but the variation would be voidable because of duress.

E   The promise to pay more money would be voidable because of duress but rescission would be barred.

Answer

The correct statement is D.

A is wrong because performance of an existing duty owed to the other party may be consideration if it confers a practical benefit.

B is wrong because even if the promise to pay more was made under duress it is only the variation that could be set aside in which case our client would be entitled to have £6,000 refunded.

C is wrong because the Company most likely exerted duress, ie made an illegitimate threat that left our client with no practical choice and was a significant reason for promising to pay more.

Finally, E is wrong because on the facts there is nothing to suggest that rescission would be barred eg by delay. Affirmation would not apply as it appears the client had to pay the total price (including the extra) in order to take delivery of the goods.

Contract

Question 2

A client, an elderly widow, consulted her bank manager ('the Manager') over plans to sell her house. The client had often sought advice from the Manager on financial matters. The Manager offered to buy the client's house at the current market estimated price. The client accepted the offer and the sale was completed eight months ago. House prices have now risen by 25% and the client wants the sale to the Manager set aside.

Which of the following best explains the legal position of the client?

A   The sale would be set aside because there was actual undue influence.

B   The relationship between the client and the Manager was based on trust and confidence and as the sale calls for an explanation it might be set aside.

C   Your client would be able to raise a presumption of undue influence but rescission would be barred as the Manager was a bona fide purchaser.

D   The sale would be set aside because it would be irrebuttably presumed that there had been undue influence exerted by the Manager.

E   For the sale to be set aside the client would have to prove undue influence and that an award of damages would be inadequate.

Answer

The correct statement is B.

A is wrong because it is unlikely on the facts that your client could establish actual undue influence.

C is wrong because for rescission to be barred by a bona fide purchaser, the bona fide purchaser must be a third party who has subsequently acquired rights in the property.

D is wrong because undue influence is never irrebuttably presumed. Some relationships are irrebuttably presumed to be fiduciary in nature eg solicitor and client.

E is wrong for two reasons – firstly, undue influence does not necessarily have to be proved (it may be presumed) and, secondly, the only remedy for undue influence is rescission (not damages too).

Question 3

A client and her husband jointly own the family house ('the house'), which is mortgaged to a bank ('the bank'). The client is disabled and cannot work but manages the family finances. The husband owns a small business. To expand the business the husband approached the bank for a loan. The bank agreed on condition it had a second charge on the house. The client was loathe to re-mortgage the house but was eventually persuaded by her husband. The bank manager went to the house to see the couple. The client said she understood the risks and signed the necessary paperwork. The husband defaulted on the loan and the bank is seeking to repossess the house.

Would the client have any ground(s) for arguing that the re-mortgage should be set aside?

A   Yes, because undue influence by the husband would be presumed and the bank had actual notice of it.

B   Yes, because undue influence would be presumed and the bank did not insist the client took independent advice.

C   Yes, because the client may be able to establish actual undue influence by the husband and that the bank had constructive notice of it.

D   No, because the bank was not put on inquiry of any undue influence and the client understood the risks.

E   No, because the wife managed the couple's finances and was aware of the risks involved in re-mortgaging the house.

Answer

C is correct. The client may be able to show actual undue influence (*Daniel v Drew*). The bank should have been put on inquiry as the relationship between the client and debtor was non-commercial and the loan was not for their joint benefit. The bank does not appear to have had a private meeting with the client to explain the risks and she did not take independent advice: so the bank would have constructive notice of the undue influence.

A and B are wrong. Undue influence would not be presumed as the relationship between client and husband was not by its nature or in fact one of trust and confidence. She managed the finances, had been loath to re-mortgage the house and said she understood the risks. Also there is no evidence the bank had actual notice of undue influence.

D is wrong. The bank should have been put on inquiry as the relationship between the client and debtor was non-commercial and the loan was not for their joint benefit.

E is wrong because there appears to have been undue influence of which the bank had constructive notice.

13 Mistake and Illegality

13.1	Mistake	142
13.2	Illegal contracts	146

SQE1 syllabus

This chapter will enable you to achieve the SQE1 assessment specification in relation to functioning legal knowledge concerned with mistake and illegality.

Note that, for SQE1, candidates are not usually required to recall specific case names or cite statutory or regulatory authorities. Cases are provided for illustrative purposes only.

Learning outcomes

By the end of this chapter you will be able to apply relevant core legal principles and rules appropriately and effectively, at the level of a competent newly qualified solicitor in practice, to realistic client-based and ethical problems and situations concerned with:

- recognising when a client may need to argue a contract is void for mistake or illegality;
- advising on the different types of mistake; and
- advising on when, and how, a contract may be illegal.

So far we have looked at vitiating factors that make a contract, or variation of a contract, voidable (ie capable of being set aside by the non-defaulting party). Now we are going to look at factors that may make a contract void from the very beginning (ie as if there had never been a contract). This is a drastic effect and so courts will only rule that a contract is void in exceptional circumstances, eg when one or both parties have made a *fundamental* mistake or the contract is contrary to public policy and illegal. Note that if a contract is voided there can be no remedy for breach (such as damages) as what the court is effectively saying is that there was no contract in the first place to breach.

13.1 Mistake

The first thing to appreciate in this area of law is that the word 'mistake' has a much more restricted meaning than in common parlance. Many examples might be given of situations where a 'mistake' in the popular sense is denied legal significance (eg because when viewed objectively the parties appeared to be in agreement) or otherwise where a remedy might be granted on some other ground such as misrepresentation. The doctrine operates only in exceptional circumstances where one party, or indeed both parties, can establish the contract was entered under a mistake that was so fundamental as to effectively negate agreement and therefore the existence of a contract.

There are basically three different types of mistake (**Figure 13.1**):

- Common mistake – where both parties have made the same fundamental mistake.
- Cross-purpose mistake – where the parties are literally at cross-purposes about some crucial aspect of the contract.
- Unilateral mistake – where only one party is mistaken, eg mistaken as to the very identity of the other contracting party.

Figure 13.1 Types of mistake

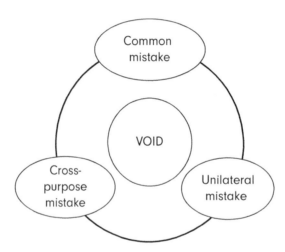

In all cases the mistake must precede the contract and have induced it.

13.1.1 Common mistake

This is sometimes known as 'identical mistake' or 'shared mistake' because both parties have made the same fundamental mistake.

As with frustration (which is a supervening rather than a preceding impossibility (**Chapter 10.2**)) there are strict limitations on the operation of common mistake:

- It will not operate if one party is at fault.
- The contract must not make express provision on the matter.
- The mistake must be fundamental, ie it must render performance of the contract impossible or radically different from what the parties anticipated.

One instance where the courts will find a fundamental mistake is where both parties are mistaken as to the very existence of the subject matter of the contract.

Example

Ruhi agrees to sell her car to Bharat, but unbeknown to either of them the car has already been destroyed in a fire. Their contract will be rendered void as there is nothing to contract about.

On the other hand, a simple mistake as to the quality of the subject matter will not usually be deemed sufficiently fundamental to affect the validity of a contract.

This is illustrated by the case of Bell v Lever Bros *[1932] AC 161. Bell and another (B and A) were made executive officers of a subsidiary of Lever Bros. The subsidiary was closed down and Lever Bros entered into contracts with B and A terminating their service contracts in return for substantial compensation. It was then discovered that B and A had previously breached their service contracts and so could have been dismissed without compensation. It was accepted that both B and A had forgotten about the earlier breaches when they entered their settlement agreements with Lever Bros.*

Lever Bros sued B and A for the return of the compensation payments on the basis that the settlement agreements were void for mistake. Both parties had wrongly thought that the service contracts had been valid; but the House of Lords said the mistake was not fundamental enough to render the settlement agreements void.

Because a mistake as to quality is unlikely to make performance radically different it is generally viewed as a last resort argument, ie where there is no other cause of action open to the claimant as was indeed the case in Bell v Lever Bros. *A and B had not lied about the status of the settlement agreement – they had genuinely (albeit conveniently) forgotten about their earlier breaches. So there had been no prospect of Lever Bros suing them for misrepresentation and/or breach of an express term of the contract. Lever Bros' only option had been to argue mistake.*

13.1.2 Cross-purpose mistake

In the case of cross-purpose mistakes, the problem is that although one or other party may assert that a contract exists, each on terms favourable to that party, objectively it is impossible to resolve the ambiguity over what was agreed. That being the case, the only possible conclusion is that there was no contract.

A classic example of a cross-purpose mistake is Raffles v Wickelhaus *(1864) 2 Hurl & C 906. It concerned a contract to sell cotton 'ex* Peerless *from Bombay', ie cotton from the ship named 'Peerless', which had sailed from Bombay. In the event there were two ships named 'Peerless' that had sailed from Bombay – one had sailed in October and the other in December. The seller brought an action against the buyer for failing to take delivery of the cotton from the ship that had sailed in December. The buyer argued there was a latent ambiguity in the contract and that they believed the ship in the contract to be the one that had sailed in October. On an objective analysis there was no way to resolve the ambiguity so the court found for the buyer, ie the contract was void.*

13.1.3 Unilateral mistake

Unilateral mistake (ie where only one party is mistaken) is often relied on where there has been a mistake as to the identity of the other contracting party. However, only a genuine mistake of this nature where the identity of the other party is of vital importance will render the contract void. If the mistake is as to anything less (eg a mistake simply as to the other party's attributes such as creditworthiness) then it will not generally affect the validity of the contract.

A case in which the identity of the other party was held to be crucial is Cundy v Lindsay *(1878) 3 App Cas 459. It involved a contract concluded by written correspondence. A rogue set up business under the name 'Blenkarn' at 37 Wood Street. A reputable company Blenkiron and Co traded at 123 Wood Street. The rogue ordered goods from the plaintiffs making his signature look like 'Blenkiron'. The plaintiffs sent the goods to 'Blenkiron and Co' at the rogue's address. Before the rogue paid for the goods, though, he resold them to innocent purchasers. The plaintiff's only hope to recover the goods was to argue mistaken identity on the basis that they intended to deal specifically with Blenkiron and Co and not with whatever firm happened to be operating from 23 Wood Street. Their argument succeeded and the contract was held to be void for mistake.*

In the above case, the plaintiffs could not rely on misrepresentation to recover the goods as rescission was barred. The goods had been resold to innocent purchasers.

The diagrams below illustrate why the plaintiffs could not rely on misrepresentation and needed to argue mistake in order to recover the goods. **Figure 13.2** shows what would have been the position if the plaintiffs had been able to rescind the contract for misrepresentation because the goods had not yet been sold to an innocent party. Title (ownership) to the goods would have reverted to the plaintiffs when the first contract was rescinded and so the innocent buyer would not have acquired title to them.

Figure 13.2 Rescission after unilateral mistake

Where, however, a bona fide purchaser has already acquired the goods (**Figure 13.3**) rescission will be barred and the bona fide purchaser will own the goods unless the plaintiffs can argue that the initial contract with the rogue was void for mistake. If the first contract is void for mistake it is as if the mistaken party never sold the car to the rogue; so the mistaken party still owns it. This was the situation in *Cundy v Lindsay.*

Figure 13.3 Bar to rescission after unilateral mistake

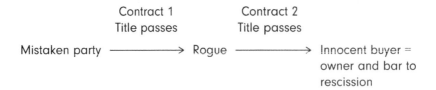

In the situation depicted by **Figure 13.3** there are two innocent parties – the mistaken party and the innocent purchaser. Only one of them will be entitled to the goods: the other will be left suing the rogue (if they can be found) for damages. The mistaken party's damages claim would be for breach of an express term and/or misrepresentation. The innocent purchaser's claim would be for breach of the statutory implied condition in contracts for the sale of goods that the seller has title to the goods that they can pass on (SGA 1979, s 12 in relation to business-to-business contracts and CRA 2015, s 17 in relation to business-to-consumer contracts). Of the two innocent parties the courts tend to have less sympathy with the mistaken party – hence why mistaken identity rarely succeeds where the deal was struck in a face-to-face situation.

As a general rule, in face-to-face situations it will be much more difficult for a person to argue they intended to deal with someone other than the person physically present in front of them.

In Lewis v Averay [1972] 1 QB 198 the plaintiff advertised his car for sale. The man who turned up claimed to be the well-known actor Richard Greene (who had played Robin Hood in a long-running TV series). He signed a cheque 'R.A. Green' and produced photographic identification in the form of an official pass for Pinewood Studios. On that basis, the plaintiff let the man take the car and log book in return for the cheque. The man then sold the car to an innocent purchaser (the defendant). The man's cheque bounced and he turned out to be a fraudster. The plaintiff's only hope of getting back his car from the defendant was to establish mistake (as rescission for misrepresentation would be barred – see **Chapter 11** and **Figure 13.3** above). But the court said the plaintiff had been more concerned about the creditworthiness of the man, rather than what he actually called himself. So it was a mistake as to an attribute (rather than identity) and as such was not fundamental enough to invalidate the contract.

13.1.4 Mistake or misrepresentation?

So if faced with a particular set of facts how do you work out whether the contract is voidable (for misrepresentation) or void (for mistake) (**Figure 13.4**)? Looking at the case law it is far from straightforward but the following guidelines can be deduced from it:

(a) If the parties are dealing face-to-face there is a strong presumption that the innocent party intends to deal with the person in front of them (ie the rogue) rather than the person they are pretending to be. As such, the contract is unlikely to be declared void for mistake although it might be rescinded for misrepresentation.

(b) Where dealings are conducted exclusively in writing, the above presumption does not apply. Instead, the written agreement must be construed to determine with whom the innocent party intended to contract. If it was with someone other than the rogue then the contract might be void for mistake.

Figure 13.4 Mistake or misrepresentation

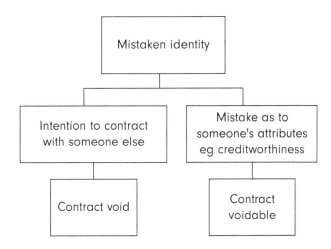

(c) The nature of the transaction may indicate to the rogue that it is vital they possess a particular attribute and if they do not do so, the offer is not addressed to them. For example, if someone orally commissions a portrait from an unknown artist passing themselves off as a famous painter, the rogue could not accept the offer: in other words there would be no contract with the rogue.

(d) If the person/entity who the rogue is pretending to be actually exists and is known to the mistaken party (eg a registered company) it suggests the offer is not addressed to the rogue. So again there could be no contract with the rogue: it would be void.

13.2 Illegal contracts

The other argument for saying a contract is void is because it is illegal. Contracts may be illegal either at the time of formation (eg because they involve the commission of a crime) or because of the way they have been performed.

A contract is illegal where its formation, purpose or performance involves the commission of a legal wrong eg breach of a statutory provision or violation of public policy. Consequently, as a general rule illegal contracts are void and courts will not allow recovery of benefits conferred in the performance of an illegal contract.

Examples of contracts that are illegal in themselves are not difficult to identify (eg a contract to commit a crime).

Some contracts, however, are formed legally but then carried out in a way that is illegal. If the illegal act is purely incidental to performance of the contract it is unlikely to affect the validity of the contract: it is enough that the wrongdoer is punished for what they did. For example a contract to deliver goods would not be voided if the driver delivering the goods was caught speeding.

 A case that illustrates this is St John Shipping Corp. v Joseph Rank Ltd *[1957] 1 QB 267. A statute made it an offence to load a ship to such an extent that the load line was below water. The offence was punishable by payment of a fine. When the plaintiff charterers committed this offence the defendants sought to withhold payment for the goods on the basis that it was an illegal contract. The court held that the statute did not prohibit contracts performed in breach of the load line rule. It was enough that the charterers should be fined for the breach.*

Where a contract is performed illegally, it is possible for either both or only one of the parties to intend illegal performance. Where both parties were aware that performance was illegal then the courts tend to take the view that neither party should be entitled to enforce the contract; the contract is void.

 This is illustrated by Ashmore, Benson, Pease & Co Ltd v AV Dawson Ltd *[1973] 1 WLR 828. The defendants agreed to transport boilers owned by the plaintiffs and did so by carrying them on lorries that could not lawfully carry them. The plaintiffs knew this to be the case. The boilers were damaged in transit and the owner sued for damages. Needless to say, the claim was rejected on the basis that the owner had effectively participated in the illegality.*

On the other hand, where one party did not know of the illegal performance of the contract by the other party, the innocent party may be able to enforce it. Clearly the illegal performer should not be permitted to enforce the contract.

13.2.1 Contracts illegal under statute

Identifying contracts that are illegal under statute is not difficult. For example, the Competition Act 1998 renders unenforceable contracts that have the effect of restricting, preventing or distorting trade within the UK.

13.2.2 Contracts illegal at common law

The courts will refuse to enforce some contracts at common law on the basis that they are contrary to public policy or morality, eg contracts that challenge the sanctity of marriage, contracts that are sexually immoral and contracts that seek to challenge the jurisdiction of the court.

Common form clauses that are prima facie void as being contrary to public policy are covenants in restraint to trade eg clauses in employment contracts restraining senior employees from working for a competitor when their employment ends or clauses in a sale and purchase agreement of a business stopping the seller setting up a competing business nearby. As a matter of public policy individuals and businesses should be able to work and operate to generate income for themselves.

However, restraints of trade may be enforceable if:

- there is a legitimate business interest to protect eg customers, employees and trade secrets; *and*
- the restraint is reasonable in terms of geographical area, duration and scope of prohibited activities.

✪ Example

NW Coaches Ltd (NWC) is a coach operator based in the north west of England. It employs a wide range of people including coach drivers, business development managers and senior executives.

In relation to the coach drivers it may be argued that NWC has no legitimate business interest to protect eg it is unlikely the coach drivers will be privy to confidential information and if they leave and work for a competitor it is unlikely to adversely affect business. So any covenants in restraint of trade in the contracts of employment of the coach drivers may well be unenforceable.

With the more senior employees, however, NWC may well have legitimate business interests to protect (eg trade secrets and goodwill) but any restraints of trade would have to be reasonable, eg limited to working for a coach operator in the north west of England for an appropriate length of time. It would be unreasonable to restrain them after termination of employment from working for a coach operator, say, based in Scotland, or otherwise from working for a 'tour operator' when the extent of NWC's business interest is coach operator. In terms of duration, the longer the duration of the restraint the more likely it is to be unreasonable but it depends on all the circumstances. For example, a reasonable period of restraint for a senior executive is going to be longer than that for a recently appointed business development manager.

13.2.3 Covenants in restraint of trade

If a restraint of trade is reasonable then the party who imposed it may apply for injunctive relief to prevent or curtail a breach (see **Chapter 9**) or otherwise apply for damages to compensate for loss suffered as a result of the breach (see **Chapter 8**), as shown in **Figure 13.5**.

Contract

Figure 13.5 Enforceability of covenants in restraint of trade

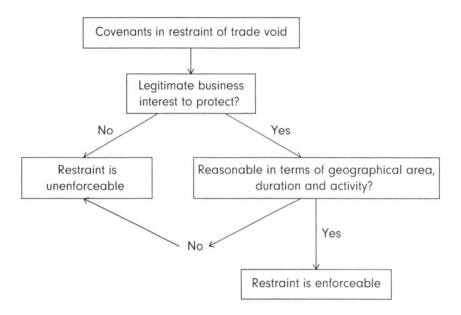

Summary

- There are three kinds of mistake: common, cross-purpose and unilateral.
- The mistake must be fundamental and precede the contract.
- The effect of mistake is to render a contract void.
- Mistake tends to be pleaded as a last resort where there is no other effective cause of action (eg there was no breach of contract or misrepresentation).
- Contracts may be illegal from the start or otherwise illegal in the way in which they are performed.
- Contracts may be illegal because they violate a statutory provision, the common law or public policy.
- As a general rule illegal contracts are unenforceable.
- Covenants in restraint of trade are prima facie void as being contrary to public policy. However, if there is a business interest to protect and the restraint is reasonable it will be enforceable.

Sample questions

Question 1

A client advertised her valuable violin for sale. Last week a man visited her and agreed to buy the violin. When he asked to pay by cheque the client hesitated and said she would prefer cash. The man said he was a famous violinist and produced photographic identification. On that basis the client accepted the cheque and let the man take the violin. Yesterday the cheque bounced and the man cannot be traced. Today the client saw the violin in the shop window of a musical instrument supplier who had bought the violin in good faith three days ago.

148

Which of the following statements best describes the client's legal position?

A   The client can rescind the contract of sale with the man based on fraudulent misrepresentation.

B   The client can recover the violin from the musical instrument supplier.

C   The client can sue the man for damages in the tort of deceit and recover the violin from the musical instrument supplier.

D   The client cannot recover the violin from the musical instrument supplier.

E   The client cannot recover the violin from the musical instrument supplier but can sue the man for damages for mistaken identity.

Answer

The correct statement is D.

A is wrong as the fact that the musical instrument supplier had purchased the violin would be a bar to rescinding the contract.

B is likely to be wrong as the client's mistake appears to be one as to attributes rather than identity.

C is wrong as rescission will be barred.

E is wrong as damages are not available for mistaken identity. The only remedy is for a court to declare the contract void.

Question 2

A baker's shop entered into a contract to bake a cake that was to be iced with a gay rights slogan. The bakers subsequently refused to bake the cake on the basis that the owners were devout Christians and they sought to refund the customer instead.

If the bakers were taken to court, which of the following would be the most likely outcome?

A   The contract was illegal as being contrary to public policy and therefore unenforceable by the customer.

B   The bakers' refusal to carry out the contract was because the customer was gay and as such amounted to unlawful discrimination and was illegal.

C   The bakers' refusal to perform the contract was legal because the bakers should not be forced to express a political opinion in which they did not believe.

D   The contract was legal and, as they had not properly performed it, the bakers should be liable to pay damages to the customer.

E   The contract was legal but the bakers' refusal to perform it as agreed was illegal because it amounted to a fundamental breach of contract.

Answer

The correct statement is C. The contract was legal and to have required the bakers to ice the slogan on the cake would have breached the bakers' human rights.

A is wrong because the contract per se was legal.

B is wrong. The bakers' refusal to perform the contract as agreed was not *because* the customer was gay. It would have required the bakers to supply a cake iced with a message with which they profoundly disagreed and that was contrary to their human rights.

D is wrong. The contract was legal but the bakers were entitled to refuse to perform it as agreed.

E is wrong. Performance of a contract will not be illegal just because it amounts to a fundamental breach of contract.

Glossary

Contract formation

Acceptance an unqualified expression of assent to the terms of the offer.

Actual authority the position where an agent acts within the powers conferred upon them by their principal.

Adequacy equivalence in value. This is **not** required to provide consideration for the other party's promise.

Agency a relationship by which one party (the agent) acts on behalf of another (the principal) with power to bind the principal to a contract with a third party.

Apparent/ostensible authority a rule that an agent (without actual authority) can bind their principal, provided the principal has represented (by words or conduct) that the agent has authority, the third party relies on the representation and, as a result, alters their position.

Battle of the forms exchange of different sets of standard conditions. The 'battle' is often won by the party that submits their standard terms last.

Bilateral a contract where consideration (in the form of promises) has been given by both parties.

Capacity the legal competence/power to enter and be bound by a contract.

Clear and unequivocal representation a statement of sufficient precision and freedom from ambiguity to ensure that the representation will be understood in the sense required, so that the representee is entitled to rely on it (in the context of promissory estoppel).

Consideration the price paid for the other party's promise, which may be the conferring of a benefit or the suffering of a detriment.

Contract for a binding contract there must be agreement, consideration and intention to create legal relations.

Counter-offer a response to an offer that introduces new or alternative terms, which has the effect of destroying the original offer.

Executed consideration act given in return for a promise.

Executory consideration promise to do or refrain from doing something.

Extinctive an effect that permanently ends legal rights (in the context of promissory estoppel).

Inequitable unfair, unjust conduct (that can undermine a defence of promissory estoppel).

Intention to create legal relations an assessment as to whether the parties intended an agreement to be legally binding based on rebuttable presumptions.

Invitation to treat an invitation to make an offer.

Offer an expression of willingness to contract on certain terms, made with the intention that it should become binding as soon as it is accepted by the person to whom it is addressed.

Offeree a person to whom an offer to enter into a contract is made by the offeror.

Offeror a person who makes an offer to enter into a contract.

Past consideration a promise made subsequent to and independent of the transaction, so making it unenforceable. But if three conditions are satisfied a past act/promise may be good consideration.

Postal rule a rule (confined to acceptances, only, using the medium of the postal service) that acceptance is effective on posting the acceptance letter, if three conditions have been complied with.

Practical benefit a benefit that is not directly provided by the other party but that arises as a result of them doing what they agreed to do, which can be sufficient to provide consideration on the variation of a contract.

Principal the party on whose behalf an agent acts.

Privity of contract only parties to the contract have rights and obligations under it.

Promisee a person to whom a promise is made.

Promisor a person who makes a promise.

Promissory estoppel an equitable doctrine that may be used in concession/downward variation cases to prevent a person from enforcing their legal rights (eg to claim outstanding debts).

Rejection a refusal to accept an offer (which includes a counter-offer), resulting in the offer being extinguished.

Reliance acting on the strength of the other party's promise or representation (eg in the context of promissory estoppel, apparent authority and misrepresentation).

Request for information a response to an offer that seeks further clarification of the terms of the offer (but which does not introduce new or alternative terms) and that does not affect the offer.

Revocation a withdrawal of an offer by offeror or reliable third party source, which can be done at any time before acceptance.

Sufficiency a promise (or act) legally recognised as providing contractual consideration for the other party's promise.

Suspensory a deferral of legal rights, which can be revived at the end of a specified period or by reasonable notice (in the context of promissory estoppel).

Unilateral a contract where only one party has made a promise and where consideration is given by the other party through them performing the required act.

Contract and remedies

Action for an agreed sum suing for money due (the price) under a contract.

Conditions important terms, the breaking of which is treated as a repudiatory breach.

Construction interpretation of the **meaning** of a contract or particular terms of a contract.

Consumer surplus/loss of amenity where there is no difference in value but the cost of cure is out of all proportion the court may award damages for loss of amenity.

Contra proferentem a rule that, where the meaning of a term is ambiguous, it will be construed against the party seeking to rely on it.

Exemption clause a clause that limits or excludes liability in some way.

Expectation loss basis awarding damages with the aim of putting the non-breaching party in the position they would have been in if the contract had been properly performed.

Guarantee secondary obligation to pay if the primary debtor defaults. Must be evidenced in writing.

Implied terms terms implied into a contract by statute, custom or because it is necessary, based on all of the relevant circumstances, to meet the parties' intentions.

Incorporation making terms part of the agreement.

Incorporation by course of dealings a sufficient number of contracts entered into by two parties, consistently on the same terms.

Incorporation by notice taking reasonable steps to make other party aware of the existence of terms before or at the time of the contract.

Indemnity primary obligation to pay. Need not be evidenced in writing.

Injunction a court order to prevent a future breach of contract.

Innominate terms terms that are neither a condition nor a warranty, where the consequences of breach depend on its effect.

Liquidated (specified) damages a genuine attempt to pre-estimate the loss that would be suffered by a breach – enforceable.

Mitigation a duty of the non-breaching party to take reasonable steps to minimise the losses arising from a breach.

Nominal damages awarded when the claimant cannot establish a loss caused by the breach.

Penalty amount stipulated is disproportionately high and designed as a threat to compel the other party to perform – unenforceable.

Quantum meruit the award of a reasonable sum for the service provided.

Reliance loss basis awarding damages with the aim of compensating the non-breaching party for expenses incurred in preparation for and in performance of the contract (which are not too remote).

Remoteness the test of whether a particular type of loss suffered as a result of a breach is outside the reasonable contemplation of the breaching party.

Repudiatory breach a breach that entitles the non-breaching party to **terminate** the contract.

Restitution a remedy aimed at preventing one party being unjustly enriched at the expense of another party.

Restraint of trade a contract that interferes with the free exercise of a person's trade/business. Prima facie void but will be upheld if reasonable.

Specific performance a court order compelling performance of contractual obligations – *ss 13–14 SGA 1979*.

Strict liability where liability arises regardless of any fault on the part of the breaching party.

Termination the non-breaching party electing to accept a repudiatory breach as bringing the contract to an end (in relation to future obligations).

UCTA 1977 reasonableness test the test to decide whether a clause was one that was fair and reasonable to include in the contract having regard to the circumstances that were (or ought reasonably to have been) known or within the contemplation of the parties at the time of the contract *s 11 and Sch. 2*.

Warranties relatively minor terms, a breach of which gives rise to damages only.

Discharge of the contract and vitiating factors

Affirmation a party acting in a way that is inconsistent with a desire to set aside a contract, in circumstances where the contract could be terminated for breach or rescinded.

Common mistake both parties have made the same fundamental mistake.

Constructive notice of undue influence where the creditor is put on inquiry of undue influence by the third party debtor AND fails to take reasonable steps to ensure the surety understands the risks/implications involved.

Cross-purpose mistake the parties are at cross-purposes and on applying the objective test of a reasonable man it is impossible to determine whether the parties intended to be bound by one set of terms or the other.

Discharge by performance where parties fully perform their part of the contract they will be discharged from the contract.

Divisible contracts – contracts that are divided into independent stages.

Doctrine of complete performance unless performance is precise and exact the contractor is not entitled to any money.

Economic duress illegitimate pressure that gives the victim no practical choice and that was a significant cause in the acceptance of the contractual variation; it allows the innocent party to rescind the (varied) contract, provided there are no bars to rescission.

False preliminary statements to be actionable in contract they must amount to breach of an express term and/or a misrepresentation.

Force majeure a clause in a contract that provides what should happen in the event of circumstances beyond the control of the parties.

Fraudulent misrepresentation a misrepresentation made knowing it to be untrue or recklessly as to whether it be true or false.

Frustration a frustrating event or change of circumstances is one that: happens after the contract was made; was unforeseen; happens without fault; and makes performance of the contract either impossible or completely different.

Illegal contracts contracts that are forbidden by statute or are contrary to public policy or the common law.

Misrepresentation a false unambiguous statement of fact made by one party to the contract to the other party that induces the other party to enter into the contract.

Non-fraudulent misrepresentation this covers misrepresentations made negligently for which damages may be available under the Misrepresentation Act 1967 and innocent misrepresentation for which there is no statutory or other right to damages.

Presumed undue influence where there is a relationship of trust and confidence (in law or in fact) AND the transaction calls for an explanation.

Repudiatory breach breach of a condition or very serious breach of an innominate term that entitles the non-defaulting party to treat the contract as at an end.

Rescission the basic remedy available where a contract is voidable, which is aimed at restoring the parties to their pre-contract position. (Note the bars to rescission.)

Substantial performance performance is complete but slightly defective. The contractor is entitled to the price less the cost of remedying the problem.

Undue influence the improper exploitation of a relationship, where one party is capable of exercising dominance over the other.

Unilateral mistake only one party has made a fundamental mistake, eg mistaken identity.

Vitiating factor something such as duress or misrepresentation that makes a contract voidable.

Void as if the contract had never been entered. The contract is a nullity.

Voidable the position where the innocent party has a right to elect to rescind or affirm the contract.

Voluntary acceptance of part performance where the innocent party has a genuine choice whether, or not, to accept part performance.

Wrongful prevention where one party in breach of contract prevents the other completing performance.

Index

Bold page numbers indicate figures, *italic* numbers indicate tables.

A

acceptance of offers
    communication of 7-9, **9**, 14-15
    defined 7
    expression of assent 8-9
    postal rule 8-9, **9**, 13
    silence 8
    terms and conditions (T&C) 8
actions for an agreed sum 88, 94
actions for the price 88
actions in debt 88
actual authority of agents 35-36
actual undue influence 131, **132**, 138-139
adequacy of consideration 22
affirmation 100, 121
agency **37**
    actual authority 35-36
    apparent authority 35-36
    authority 35-37, 38-39
    commercial law 34, 35-37
    commercial/legal use of term 35
    examples 34, 35
    need for agents 35
    principals 35
    third parties 35, 36
amenity, loss of 83
apparent authority of agents 35-36
apparent/ostensible authority 35-36
auctions, offers and 6-7, 14
authority of agents 35-37, 38-39

B

bargain, loss of 78-79, 86
'battle of the forms' 8
bilateral contracts 22
buyer beware 118, 125

C

capacity to make a contract
    corporations 42, 43-44
    Limited Liability partnerships 44
    mental incapacity 43
    minors **42**, 42-43, 44-45
    necessaries 42, 44-45
    statutory corporations 44
certainty 11-12
classification of terms 51-52, **53**
clear and unequivocal representation 151
commercial agreements, intention to create legal relations and 18-19, 20
common intention of the parties 116
common law
    rules, exemption clauses and 64-65
    terms implied at 54, 61
common mistake **142**, 142-143
communication of acceptance of offers 7-9, **9**, 14-15
companies, capacity to make a contract of 43-44
complete performance doctrine 106-108, **109**, 110
completeness 11-12
conditions 51-52, 53, 56, 100
consideration
    adequacy of 22
    alteration promises to pay less 26-28, **28**
    alteration promises to pay more 24-26, **25**, 29
    contractual variations 24-28, **25**, 28, 29-30
    defined 22
    economic duress and 130-131
    executed 22
    executory 22
    past 23
    promissory estoppel 26-28, 30
    requirements **24**
    sufficiency of 22-23, 26, 31
    total failure of 89-90
    variations, contractual 24-28, **25**, **28**
construction 152
    exemption clauses 64-65
consumer surplus 83
contents of contracts *see* exemption clauses; terms and conditions (T&C)
contra proferentem rule 64-65
contractual variations, consideration and 24-28, **25**, 28, 29-30
corporations, capacity to make a contract and 42, 43-44

Index

cost of cure 82–83, 85
counter-offers 8
cross-purpose mistake **142**, 143
custom, terms implied by 54

D

damages
    breach of contract as cause of 78
    cost of cure 82–83
    expectation loss 78–79, 95
    fraudulent misrepresentation 119
    idea of 78
    innocent misrepresentation 121
    limitations on awards of 80–82, **84**
    liquidated damages clauses 83–84
    loss of bargain 78–79, 86
    mitigation of loss 82, 84, 86, 95
    negligent misrepresentation 120
    negotiating damages 92, 94, 95
    nominal 78
    penalty clauses 83–84
    quantification of 82–83
    reliance loss 79
    remoteness of damage 80–81, **81**, 84
    restitutionary 91–92
    specified damages clauses 83–84
    substantial 78
    types of loss recoverable 80, 84
    wrongful prevention 107–108
delays
    as bar to rescission 121–122
    frustration 103
discharge by performance 106–108, **109**, 110
divisible obligations 107
domestic agreements, intention to create legal relations and 19, *19*
drunkenness, capacity to make a contract and 43
duress 137
    consideration, economic duress and 130–131
    economic/business threats 128–129, 130–131
    effects of 129–130
    improper/illegitimate threats 128–129
    physical violence 128
    practical benefit 130, 137
    rescission 129–130
    voidable, contracts as due to 128

E

equitable remedies
    injunction 88–89
    rescission 121–122
    specific performance 88
evidenced in writing 93
executed consideration 22
executory consideration 22
exemption clauses 51
    common law rules 64–65
    construction 64–65
    Consumer Rights Act 2015 68–69, 73
    contra proferentem rule 64–65
    as hidden in small print 64
    incorporation 64
    incorporation of terms 64
    reasonable notice of a term 51
    reasonableness test 66–67, 71–72
    sales contracts 68
    service contracts 69
    statutory controls 65–69
    third parties 69–70
    Unfair Contract Terms Act 1977 65–68, **66**, 70
expectation loss 78–79, 95
express terms 50–53
expression 4
expression of assent 8–9
extinctive 151

F

fact, terms implied in 54
false preliminary statements 116
fiduciary relationships, undue influence and 131
'force majeure' clauses 104
fraudulent misrepresentation 119–120, 122, 124–125
frustration
    circumstances for 101
    consequences of 104–105
    defined 101, **101**
    delays 103
    event beyond control of either party 104
    'force majeure' clauses 104
    Law Reform (Frustrated Contracts) Act (LR(FC)A) 1943 104–105
    radically different 102–103
    something unexpected 103–104
    unforeseen events 101, 103–104, 111–112

G

glossary 151–154
goods, consumers' rights to enforce terms about 58
goods on display, invitation to treat and 5
guarantees 92–93, **93**

I

identical mistake 142–143
'If' contracts *see* unilateral contracts
illegal contracts 149–150
    at common law 147
    covenants in restraint of trade 147, **148**
    defined 146
    under statute 147
implied terms
    common law, terms implied at 54, 61
    Consumer Rights Act 2015 *57*, 58–59, 62
    custom, terms implied by 54
    defined 54
    fact, terms implied in 54
    law, terms implied in 54
    Sale of Goods Act 1979 *55*, 55–56
    statute, terms implied by 55–59, 60–61
    Supply of Goods and Services Act 1982 *56–57*
incorporation
    by course of dealings 152
    exemption clauses 64
    by notice 152
    of terms 50–51, **52**
indemnities 93, **93**
inebriation, capacity to make a contract and 43
inequitable 151
injunction 88–89
innocent misrepresentation 120–121
innominate terms 53, 61, 100, 107
intention (definition of offer) 4
intention to create legal relations **18**
    commercial agreements 18–19, 20
    defined 18
    domestic agreements 19, *19*
    rebuttable presumptions 18, 19, 31
intermediate terms 53
invitation to treat 5
    advertisements 5
    goods on display 5
    tenders 7

L

lapse of time 11
law, terms implied in 54
Limited Liability partnerships, capacity to make a contract and 44
liquidated damages clauses 83–84
loss
    of amenity 83
    of bargain 78–79, 86
    consumer surplus 83
    expectation loss 78–79
    mitigation of loss 82, 84, 86
    pecuniary/non-pecuniary 80
    of profit 78–79, 86
    quantification of damages 82–83
    reliance loss 79
    remoteness of damage 80–81, **81**
    types of loss recoverable 80, 84

M

measurement of damages 82–83
mental incapacity, capacity to make a contract and 43
minors, capacity to make a contract and **42**, 42–43, 44–45
misrepresentation
    buyer beware 118, 125
    categories of pre-contract statements 116–118
    common intention of the parties 116
    definition 118–119
    fraudulent 119–120, 122, 124–125
    innocent 120–121
    misleading statements 116
    Misrepresentation Act (MA) 1967 120
    negligent 120
    or mistake **145**, 145–146
    outcomes of **123**
    rescission 121–122, 124–125
    statement inducing other party to enter into contract 119
    statement made by one party to the other 119
    statement of fact 118–119
    types of 119–121
    untrue statement 118
    see also duress; undue influence
mistake
    common **142**, 142–143
    cross-purpose **142**, 143
    definition in law 142
    identity of other contracting party 143–145, 149
    or misrepresentation **145**, 145–146
    types of **142**
    unilateral **142**, 143–145
mitigation of loss 82, 84, 86, 95

N

nature of the document 50
necessaries 42, 44–45
negligent misrepresentation 120

Index

negotiating damages 92, 94, 95
nominal damages 78
non-fraudulent misrepresentation 120
non-pecuniary loss 80
notice of revocation 10–11

O

offerees 4
offerors 4
offers
    acceptance 7–9
    adverts of reward 5
    auctions 6–7, 14
    counter-offers 8
    defined 4–5
    expression 4
    intention 4
    invitation to treat 5
    the person to whom it is addressed 4–5
    termination of **9**, 9–11
onerous terms 50–51

P

parties
    agency 34, 35–37, **37**
    Contracts (Rights of Third Parties) Act 1999 34–35
    importance of determining 34
    privity of contract 34
    third parties 34–35
past consideration 23
pecuniary/non-pecuniary loss 80
penalty clauses 83–84
postal rule 8–9, 13
practical benefit 130, 137
pre-contract statements, categories of 116–118
preliminary statements, categories of 116–118
presumed undue influence 131, 132, **132**
previous consistent course of dealing 51, 64
principals 35
privity of contract 34
profit, loss of 78–79, 86
promisee 151
promisor 151
promissory estoppel 26–28, 30
public policy 23

Q

quantification of damages 82–83
quantum meruit 152

R

radically different 102–103
reasonable notice of a term 50–51, 64
reasonableness test, exemption clauses and 66–67, 71–72
rebuttable presumptions 18, 19, 31
registered companies, capacity to make a contract and 43
rejection of offer by offeree 10
reliance 152
reliance loss 79
remedies
    actions for an agreed sum 88, 94
    broken contract 90
    damages, restitutionary 91–92
    defendant to perform contract 88–89
    guarantees 92–93, **93**
    indemnities 93, **93**
    injunction 88–89
    recovery of money due to total failure of consideration 89–90, 95
    restitution 89–92
    specific performance 88
    unformed contract 90–91
    see also damages
remoteness of damage 80–81, **81**, 84
representations *see* misrepresentation
repudiatory breaches 100
request for information 152
rescission 121–122, 124–125
    duress 129–130
    undue influence 131
    unilateral mistake 144
reserve prices at auctions 6
restitution 89–92
    wrongful prevention 107–108
restraint of trade 147, 153
revocation of offers 10–11

S

sales contracts, exemption clauses in 68
service contracts, exemption clauses in 69
services/work, consumers' rights to enforce terms about 59
'setting aside' a contract 121–122
shared mistake 142–143
signatures 64
    terms and conditions (T&C) 50
silence as acceptance of offers 8
specific performance 88
specified damages clauses 83–84

statute, terms implied by 55–59
statutory corporations, capacity to make a contract and 44
strict liability 56
substantial damages 78
substantial performance 107, 110
sufficiency of consideration 22, 26, 31
suspensory 152

T

tenders, invitation to treat and 7
termination of contracts
    affirmation 100
    breach of condition 100
    breach of contract, consequences of **100**
    complete performance doctrine 106–108, **109**
    discharge by performance 106–108, **109**, 110
    discharge of parties from obligations 101
    frustration 101–106, 111–112
    innominate term, breach of 100
    repudiatory breaches 100
    right to 100
    terms and conditions (T&C) 51–53
termination of offers **9**
    lapse of time 11
    rejection by offeree 10
    revocation 10–11
terms and conditions (T&C) 8, **60**
    classification of terms 51–52, **53**
    common law, terms implied at 54
    conditions 51–52, 53, 56
    Consumer Rights Act 2015 *57*, 58–59
    custom, terms implied by 54
    drawing of attention to 51
    exemption clause 51
    fact, terms implied in 54
    goods, consumers' rights to enforce terms about 58
    implied terms 54–59, 60–62
    incorporation of terms 50–51, **52**
    innominate terms 53, 61
    intermediate terms 53
    law, terms implied in 54
    nature of the document 50
    onerous terms 50–51
    previous consistent course of dealing 51, 64
    reasonable notice 50–51, 64
    Sale of Goods Act 1979 *55*, 55–56
    services/work, consumers' rights to enforce terms about 59
    signatures 50, 64
    statute, terms implied by 55–59
    Supply of Goods and Services Act 1982 *56–57*, 70
    termination of contracts 51–53
    timing of notice 50
    warranties 51, 52–53
terms of a contract
    express terms 50–53
    implied terms 54–61, *55, 56–57*
third parties
    agency 35, 36
    Contracts (Rights of Third Parties) Act 1999 34–35, 69–70
    exemption clauses 69–70
    undue influence 133–135, **136**
timing of notice of a term 50
total failure of consideration 89–90, 95

U

undue influence
    actual 131, **132**, 138–139
    constructive notice of 134, 139
    deciding **133**
    definition 131
    presumed 131, 132, **132**
    put on inquiry 135
    reasonable steps 135
    rebuttable, presumption of as 132
    relationship of trust and confidence 131, 132, 138
    rescission 131
    third parties 133–135, **136**
    transaction must call for an explanation 132
    voidable, contracts as due to 128
unforeseen events 101, 103–104, 111–112
unilateral contracts 5, 6, 10, 14, 22
unilateral mistake **142**, 143–145
unqualified expression of assent 7, 8

V

variations, contractual, consideration and 24–28, **25**, 28, 29–30
vitiating factors 154
    see also duress; illegal contracts; misrepresentation; mistake; undue influence

voidable contracts 154
    see also duress; illegal contracts; misrepresentation; mistake; undue influence
voluntary acceptance of part performance 108

W

warranties 51, 52-53
wrongful prevention 107-108